THE GENERAL

THE GENERAL
John Boorman

ff

faber and faber

First published in 1998
by Faber and Faber Limited
3 Queen Square London WCIN 3AU

Photoset by Parker Typesetting Service, Leicester
Printed in England by Clays Ltd, St Ives plc

John Boorman is hereby identified as author of this
work in accordance with Section 77 of the Copyright,
Designs and Patents Act 1988

A CIP record for this book
is available from the British Library
ISBN 0-571-19646-2

2 4 6 8 10 9 7 5 3 1

CONTENTS

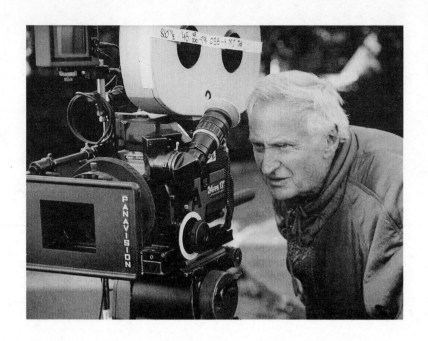

INTRODUCTION

THE HUNT FOR CAHILL

You could not live in Ireland in the eighties and be unaware of Martin Cahill, mastermind of daring robberies culminating in the theft of paintings from the collection of Sir Alfred Beit, including the only Vermeer in private hands. Despite being the police's most wanted man, he artfully eluded detection and capture. Confronted by photographers, he covered his face with his hand or with one of his range of designer balaclavas. Blurred, fleeting images of him appeared in the press, but what he really looked like, his countenance, his character, remained an enigma. His exploits went from the outrageous to the bizarre. When he needed weapons, he robbed them from the police arsenal. If there was a criminal case being prepared against him or members of his gang, he broke into the office of the Director of Public Prosecutions and stole the files.

Police embarrassment became political outrage and a task force of ninety men was assigned to an unprecedented round-the-clock surveillance in a desperate attempt to ensnare him. While the police fumed and the politicians ranted, the ordinary Dubliner had a sneaking admiration for the almighty cheek of the man.

At this point he was being hounded, not only by the police, but also by the press, and finally a TV reporter waylaid him as he made his weekly visit to collect his unemployment benefit. He was shadowed by two Gardai and although he kept his face covered, we finally got a vivid impression of Martin Cahill. A small, fat fellow with balding reddish-blond hair, he answered questions with a teasing wit:

'How do you feel about the police following you everywhere?'

'There's no police following me. I don't see them.' (They were inches from his shoulder.)

'Do you deny you are Martin Cahill, known as the General, wanted for armed robbery?'

'Must be some other Martin Cahill.'

'Who do you think is the General?'

'Some army officer?' Said in a high-pitched voice of mock innocence – the schoolboy denying guilt to a Christian Brother.

Having spent twenty-five enchanted, exasperated years in Ireland, I instantly recognized the manner, honed in surviving the oppression of two colonizing powers, the English and the Church. A role is assumed, a cover story concocted and the play-acting conceals a contempt for authority, a rage at perceived injustice, a ferocious cunning, a sense of perpetual celebration, a dark brutality – in fact the pagan characteristics of a Celtic chieftain. The public (and my own) fascination with Cahill probably drew on something archetypal from the deep past, a relish and envy for the freedom of one who dares defy the might of society. It brought to mind those Irish gang bosses in Chicago. They came out of the same mould as Cahill. The popular appeal of *The Godfather* was that it offered a tribal social structure, rather than the perplexing and frustrating complexities of a modern democracy. Only a few hundred years back we were all living in tribes and, emotionally, it seems that we have hardly graduated from that condition.

Facts on Cahill were scant enough, but the crime reporter Paul Williams spent years tracking him down as remorselessly as the cops. The more slippery Cahill was, the more determined was Williams. Eventually he published his account in a book entitled *The General*. I bought it and devoured its contents. It was more bizarre than anything one could imagine. It emerged that he lived amicably with two sisters and fathered a number of children with both of them. He did not smoke or drink or drug. Apart from his love of expensive motorbikes, he lived simply, even frugally. He took his pleasure from making fools of the police, the Church, civil servants and even the IRA, which he despised, not on moral or political grounds, but because it was another institution, for it was institutions of all complexions that were the focus of Cahill's ire.

THE RIGHTS

I had been thinking for some time about making a film about contemporary Ireland, a country shaking off its Catholic past and fumbling towards an uncertain future in Europe. This story seemed to afford the opportunity.

To my horror I found that the film rights had been acquired by a smart young American, P. J. Pettite. My partner in Merlin Films, Kieran Corrigan, and I approached him. He was pleased that I wanted to direct it, but was so possessive and afraid that he would lose control that he insisted on a long-form production and distribution agreement before I could start work on a script. Usually a short-form agreement is drawn up that summarizes the main issues. The final 70-page contract is complex and time-consuming, and is often not completed until the picture has been shot and edited. Negotiations stretched over many months and eventually got so mired in trivial detail that I threw in the towel and left the ring.

I turned my attention to C. S. Lewis' *The Lion, the Witch and the Wardrobe*, a project that involved Animatronics and computer-generated imagery on a large scale. Working with the brilliant designer Jim Acheson, we story-boarded the entire film, more than 2,500 drawings. We built models of the sets and supervised the construction of a range of creatures at the Jim Henson Workshop. The budget came out at $85 million and Paramount demurred. Nine months of work. On the rebound I rushed headlong into a low-budget movie, *A Simple Plan*. This foundered two weeks from principal photography, due to a dispute between the producer and Paramount's financing partner.

I got back to Ireland to discover that P. J. Pettite was ready to sell his rights without strings. It transpired that he had negotiated with another Irish film company, Little Bird. They had also failed to come to terms and decided to make their own version of the story without P. J. or the book. In buying the rights we found that we had also inherited his legal action against Little Bird, attempting to restrain them from using material from the book. I also discovered that they had a script written and had gained some financial support already. It became apparent why P. J. had suddenly become so ready to sell. I had to move fast. It was March 1997.

SCRIPT, CAST AND BUDGET

I buried myself in all the available research. Paul Williams supplied additional information not included in the book. As I shaped the material, I had to decide how the characters spoke, related to each other, their preoccupations. The gang members were shadowy enough – I simply invented a group of characters and gave them the names of people in my village. Cahill himself sprung to life on the page. I had heard his voice. I knew his wiles. Frances Cahill and her sister Tina were a more difficult problem. They were not involved in criminal activities. Did I have the right to depict them? And in what light? I considered contacting them. Paul Williams advised against it. He said they would refuse any contact with anyone outside their world.

This was to be a fiction based on fact. The framework would be built of incidents that occurred. Beyond that I would rely on the truth of the imagination. I wrote the first draft in three weeks. Our strategy was to have a script and budget ready for the Cannes Film Festival in May. We just about managed it.

My agents Ken Kamins and Jeff Berg circulated the script to buyers on the Croissette, and Kieran and I pitched it furiously. As ever, the question came back, 'Who's in it?' Gabriel Byrne was suggested, as was Gary Oldman, both actors I admire greatly – except that I desperately wanted to cast Brendan Gleeson. Apart

Brendan Gleeson

from an uncanny resemblance to Cahill, Brendan is one of those rare actors capable of possessing a character in a way that seems to transcend acting. I have followed his career closely. He first came to my attention as Michael Collins in the TV film *The Treaty*. He was Mel Gibson's bearded side-kick in *Braveheart* and the dim-witted thug in *I Went Down*. The *Irish Times* critic Michael Dwyer has aptly described him as the Irish Depardieu. Needless to say, my decision to cast him caused dismay among potential investors.

Simon Perry of British Screen expressed great enthusiasm for the script and it led me to hope that for the first time in my career I might get some money from Britain. Perry suddenly back-peddled. He had offered support to the Little Bird project and felt himself in a dilemma. He said he could not invest in both, and how could he choose between them? When he learnt there was a legal dispute between the parties, he announced that he could not possibly consider investing until these matters had been resolved. He was off the hook. Fortunately, the Irish Film Board took a more relaxed position. They saw no impediment to backing both projects and promised us £400,000.

At the end of Cannes, despite widespread admiration for the script, no one had stepped up.

Back in Ireland, Kieran put together Section 35 investors which provided us with around $1 million. He then persuaded a group of private investors to take the UK and Irish rights for a further $1 million.

I threw myself at the feet of Paul Rassam, the distinguished French distributor who had done well with my films in the past. He pleaded for some name casting. I could not oblige. He hesitated. I could not reach him on the phone. Bad sign. Meanwhile, Kieran engineered an offer from a French producer who was prepared to finance the picture fully, but his terms were so wretched that it was extremely unlikely that we would ever see profits, irrespective of how well the film performed, and since I was deferring all my fees as writer, director and producer this was singularly unattractive. However, if there was nothing else on offer, I was ready to take the deal because at least I would get to make the picture. This was important to me after the frustrations of the last two years. My career was in disarray. I needed to make a movie to stay in the game.

J&M Entertainment, the sales agents, agreed to prepare estimates of the figures they felt they could raise from territories around the world and Kieran took these to a number of banks in an attempt to raise the balance of the budget. It became clear that they would require at least one major distributor to be in place before they would lend, something that would verify J&M's confidence. The casting issue kept coming back at me. Could I cast star names in any of the other roles? Well, no, I couldn't, not the way I saw the film.

I renewed my efforts to reach Paul. I left many messages: the ship was about to sail, the train was leaving the station, there was still time for him to book a passage, a seat, an honoured place at the table. His silence was ominous.

THE RACE

Whether a major studio is involved or you are piecing a picture together independently – as we were here – there is never a moment when someone says, 'Right, here's the money, go make your movie.' Approval of budget, cast and script are withheld until the very last. But there comes a time when, unless you seize the moment, make the assumption that it will somehow come together, it will disintegrate into an endless series of less and less convincing meetings. Confidence is all. You have to be seen to be making the movie.

By any measure, that moment had not arrived. But there was another imperative. I had to start before my rivals. They were months ahead of me. If they were able to announce a start date before me, I knew my version would not be made. I took the plunge, hired Jina Jay to cast the film, took on Jo Homewood as production manager, and booked Seamus Deasy as cameraman. Kieran and I swallowed hard and put our own money at risk.

Several nervous British banks flirted then skittered away. How do they manage to run up so many bad loans when they are this cautious? Kieran took off for LA to negotiate with more adventurous US banks, including Coamerica Bank which was just beginning to move into film financing.

Paul called. 'I'm on the train,' he said, 'for one million dollars'. Bless him. I got the news to Kieran. His position with the bank was radically improved.

Derek Wallace was a resourceful propman who had worked on a number of projects with me. I gave him the job of designing the picture. No one better – on a tight budget – to forage, beg, borrow and steal the sets and locations we needed. He has an ability to find imaginative solutions to intractable problems, a practical dreamer.

Con Cremins came on board as accountant. He was with me in the Amazon; a great man to have at your back holding the fiscal line. We refined the budget and Con, Jo and I travelled to London to seek a completion bond with Film Finances. Despite their title, the one thing they don't do is finance films. They take a large fee to assure investors that if the picture goes wildly over budget they will provide the extra money. They insist that a 10 per cent contingency is added to the budget and their conditions for paying up are so draconian that investors usually prefer to stump up the extra money themselves. However, with several partners involved, a bond is an essential instrument in giving legal comfort to the investors. Film Finances' tooth-comb found no flaws in our estimates, but they put their corporate finger on two potential problems. What if the criminal community disrupted filming, resulting in expensive delays. I pointed out that we had put in substantial sums for security and protection. 'What if', they added nervously, 'you fall out with Merlin films and they replace you as director? Since you are receiving no fee, there is no money in the budget to pay a successor.' I was able to point out that I owned 51 per cent of Merlin Films, so the only person who could fire me was me. If I died or was incapacitated, the insurance company would stump up. We got our bond.

However, I was concerned about security, more than I was prepared to admit to Film Finances. An unscrupulous journalist on *The Sunday Times* had procured a copy of the script and written a piece accusing me of glamorizing violence and torture, the first time I had a film reviewed before it was made. The Irish tabloids picked up the story and began running fabricated variations, embroidering on what their rivals had written: people's lives were being threatened if they took jobs on the movie; we were the victims of every imaginable intimidation. All this was totally untrue. At this point we had no contact of any kind with the criminal element. However, the press stories were creating problems. It was proving

xiii

difficult to secure locations – owners were afraid of being burnt or bombed or worse. Our lawyer wrote to all the papers threatening legal action if they persisted in printing false and unsubstantiated stories. It quietened them down.

ENTER GERRY O'CARROLL

In searching for someone to help us, I met a man who was to have a profound effect on the film – Detective Inspector Gerry O'Carroll. He was one of several senior policemen who had hunted down Cahill. He knew him well, knew the members of his gang, knew his family. I spent hours talking with him and he gave me fresh insights into the character. Gerry is the most compelling raconteur and he brought the subject to vivid life for me from another perspective. Like so many of Dublin's police he was from the country, in his case the border land between Cork and Kerry. It has long been the policy of the Gardai to police districts with men from elsewhere. As a result, Dublin policemen are often lonely and isolated and dependent on each other for social comfort. They feel under siege from a hostile community, particularly in the rougher sections. This was not the case with Gerry. He has both a warmth and an intimidating power that gained him friends and respect. He is famed for venturing alone into no-go areas with impunity. His welcoming smile is offset by his bone-crunching handshake which reminds you of the great strength of a man not to be trifled with.

He briefed me on the current gangland situation in Dublin. Over the last twenty years the Gardai had been stretched to the limit dealing with armed terrorist organizations which raised much of their finance though bank raids and kidnapping. There was widespread sympathy for the aims of the IRA in the Republic, even by many policemen, or at the very least a reluctance to inform on them. This made it difficult to get convictions. The terrorists were well organized and heavily armed and for many years the police carried no weapons.

It was in this environment that several armed gangs flourished. Weapons were easy to obtain. There was often overlap between criminals and subversives.

Then came the shocking assassination of the crime reporter

Veronica Guerin. This caused such an international furore (not to mention a hail of film scripts) that there was suddenly the political will to do something about the situation. A drastic bill was hurriedly passed into law which gave the police enormous powers to confiscate property of suspected drug traffickers and criminals. This police were issued with modern automatic weapons and a wholesale assault on the gangs was mounted. Cahill's gang had fallen apart after his death in 1994, but there were others, more ruthless than he had been and mostly involved in drugs.

As a result, the criminals were in full retreat. Many of them were skulking in Spain or Miami, waiting for the heat to cool before they returned. War had also broken out between the gangs that remained and they could be relied upon to kill each other at regular intervals. In the light of all this, Gerry felt we had a good chance of being left alone, although he cautioned that there was always some psychopath wanting to make a name for himself.

LEGAL BATTLES

At this point, however, I was under more threat from the lawyers than from the criminals. A bevy of legal experts was poring over my script. Before the bank would sign up there were more hurdles to leap. We had to get errors and omissions insurance (E&O). Before they would give us cover they wanted to be absolutely certain that there *were* no errors or omissions, that no one could sue for libel or defamation or plagiarism or anything else. One of them rebuked me with the remark, 'There's something in here to offend everybody.' Like the completion bond people, they only wanted to play if there was no chance of losing.

The dead can't sue, so we were safe with Cahill and the members of his gang who had succumbed to drug overdoses or come to other sticky ends. It was thought that even if some criminals claimed to recognize themselves, it would be difficult for them to sue for defamation, unless they felt I had depicted them too mildly and thus damaged their reputations for ferocity. I had to make sure that Frances and Tina were not seen to be privy to any criminal acts and, most importantly, that no lawyers, judges or policemen could recognize themselves. The most litigious people, I was warned, were those whose business was the law. A careful check was made on names I had invented to make sure they did not correspond to any real-life actors in the Cahill drama. I fought them every inch of the way, but in the end I was forced to make a hundred little snips and tucks, dulling some of my sharpest lines. There was one particularly good epigram that I put in the mouth of a judge which turned out to be exactly what a certain judge had said. I regretted losing that one.

Finally we scraped through. Kieran was able to write another paragraph into the contract with the bank and edge closer to a deal.

PRE-PRODUCTION

I was in full pre-production. Kevan Barker, an experienced production manager and producer in his own right, agreed to come on as first assistant. We were searching for locations, trying to reassure people that no harm would befall them. One piece of good fortune: Jim Sheridan had renovated a derelict slum for his film *The Boxer* and he was willing to let me take it over and transform it into Hollyfield, the doleful housing estate where Cahill grew up.

Brendan and I began to build Cahill's character. We were determined not to flinch from showing his ruthless brutality as well as his wit and cleverness. Would the audience recoil and find him unsympathetic? I hoped so. But interesting. Fascinating. Nor did we want it to be like *Scarface*, where the audience is somehow invited to enjoy the sadism. We agreed that we should tell the truth about him unflinchingly. We would be careful not to appeal for audience sympathy and to show the beastliness without relish or decoration. I made two crucial decisions about the style of the film: first, I would show his assassination by the IRA at the opening of the picture. This knowledge would then cast a shadow across the rest of the movie. His life, his hardships and his despicable acts would assume, I hoped, a tragic dimension. I know that it is said cynically that Hollywood likes tragedies with a happy ending, but this had to be truly tragic. I kept telling everyone: this is nothing if it is not a tragedy. The tragedy of a bad man who could have been good, could have lived, could have known greatness.

The second decision was that the film would be in black and white. Why? For a number of reasons. Eastman and Fuji colour films are too saturated. They prettify. They vulgarize. And in particular, they romanticize poverty. Directors and cameramen struggle with this problem – using deep shadow, low-key lighting to dull the hues, pre- and post-flashing to soften the colours, attempting to control the palette by keeping the sets and costumes within a narrow colour range. In *Point Blank* I shot each scene in a single colour, a monotone, in fact. The head of the art department at MGM wrote a memo predicting disaster: 'He has a green office with green furniture, there are seven men in green suits with green shirts and green ties. This movie will be laughed off the screen.' I reminded him of Magritte's painting of a pipe on which is written: 'This is not a pipe.' Film is not life. In that office scene the colours were perceived not only as shades of green, but as browns and yellows, even blacks. The eye saw harmony and subtle nuances. No one, no critic ever referred to it. In that film I was using colour, but seeking the unifying effect of black and white. Black and white abstracts while colour distracts, detracts from the faces of the actors, diminishes intensity. In *The General* there were many street scenes where I could not control the colour, streets drenched in the lurid poly-plastic colours of the contemporary world – acid-yellow anoraks, brick-red Toyotas, electric-blue neon lights. In black and white I could eliminate these distractions. But there are deeper reasons. Most of us dream in black and white, remember in black and white. A black and white film approaches the condition of dream, of memory, reaches out into the audience's unconscious. There was often a mythic dimension to black and white movies. They presented a familiar yet alien world, a contiguous reality.

I asked my cameraman, Seamus Deasey, to shoot tests. We experimented with both black and white and with colour stock which we had the lab print in black and white. We chose the latter option because the black and white stocks available are very limited. We found there was no loss of quality in going from colour to black and white. The real challenge for Seamus was to adjust his style of lighting. Like every other modern cameraman he uses mostly soft, indirect light bouncing off sheets of polystyrene or Chinese lanterns giving a flattering glow to faces, relying on the gradations of colour to separate the various levels and objects. In black and white the planes must be differentiated by shafts of direct light. Objects need back light to rim their contours. It is more complex and time-consuming. It is also something of a lost art. Like me, Seamus is old enough to have shot a lot of black and white before colour came along, and he began to dust off his technique.

CASTING

We had more than seventy speaking parts. In London and Dublin, Jina and I saw every available Irish actor. I was very lucky to persuade many distinguished actors to play small roles. There is a plethora of talent at present. I was spoilt for choice. Sean McGinley and Adrian Dunbar signed up for leading parts. Eamon Owens, the eponymous hero of Neil Jordan's *The Butcher Boy*, became the young Martin Cahill. One role proved hard to cast,

John Boorman with Jon Voight

the police inspector who is Cahill's foe, admirer, nemesis. There were a limited number of scenes in which to develop the relationship and it required a powerful actor who could match the dynamics of Gleeson. *In extremis* I turned to my old friend Jon Voight. He is one of the very few American actors with a consummate skill for accents. I called him up, sent him the script. He agreed without hesitation. He arrived for rehearsals with some trepidation. He was, after all, surrounded by actors who belonged to the milieu, who were born to it.

I said, 'Jon, there's someone I want you to meet.' I introduced Detective Inspector Gerry O'Carroll. They became inseparable. Jon was soon talking with Gerry's accent as they toured the streets and police stations. Jon sat in on interrogations. He listened, entranced, to Gerry's stories. He wanted Gerry to be present when he shot his scenes to correct any slips. Gerry complied. It emerged that he was a serious movie buff.

THE RACE HOTS UP

I had set a start date for 10 August. Kieran suggested we should delay it since the deal was still not in place. He was on the phone to LA night after night, talking to the bank and its lawyers who seemed to be dragging things out. In the meantime we were funding the picture ourselves and we had spent more than £250,000, breaking the first rule of film producing: never use your own money. Perhaps we should stop making further commitments until the deal was in place. We considered it carefully, but decided not to lose momentum. We had overtaken our rivals. They were threatening to start in October. I did not want them to close the gap. We pressed on.

Rehearsals were intensely exciting. Sparks flew between Jon and Brendan, both enormously inventive actors. I integrated several of their improvisations into the script. Adrian and Sean added shafts of wit and insight as their characters took form. The women, Maria Doyle Kennedy (Frances) and Angeline Ball (Tina), brought passion and warmth to my words. We discussed the difficulties of impersonating living characters. Brendan wrote to Frances Cahill saying that he would try to do justice to her husband. There was no reply. I did, however, receive an articulate

Maria Doyle Kennedy with Angeline Ball

and touching letter from Martin Cahill junior. I showed it to
Gerry. He said the boy was a highly intelligent art student with no
involvement in crime. Martin felt his family had been pilloried in
the tabloid press and that it was difficult for them to try to lead
normal lives. He recognized the legitimacy of our making the film,
but asked not to be included in it. I replied, complying with his
wish, and expressed the hope that the film would be cathartic
rather than painful to the family. I invited him to visit the set but
he did not respond.

Ten days to our start date, a bombshell. Little Bird delivered a
summons late on a Friday for us to answer in court on the
following Monday. They were seeking an injunction to prevent us
from shooting our picture. Paul Williams quotes in his book from
interviews with Cahill conducted by Michael O'Higgins, a one-
time journalist, now a barrister. It appeared that Little Bird had
cleverly acquired the film rights to those interviews and was
seeking to prevent us from using any material that might have
derived from them, thus neatly turning the tables on us.

I spent the weekend analysing my script and providing our
lawyers with an account of my sources for every single scene in the

film. We concluded there was nothing drawn from O'Higgins' material. We worked through Sunday night. Williams went through his mountainous files verifying *his* sources. We were still completing our depositions on Monday morning. Bleary-eyed, we staggered into court. Kieran, a barrister himself, had organized the whole operation with great aplomb. He is at his best under fire, comfortable in crisis. He admired the cunning of our adversary's strategy. This was the last week before the courts rose for the summer recess. They had timed it thus in the hope and expectation that the case would be adjourned and not heard until the new term in October. With an injunction hanging over us, we would not qualify for our E&O insurance and therefore would not be able to conclude our bank deal. Little Bird would have caught up. Kieran's thrust in preparing our case was to show the judge there had been no plagiarism. And even if there was a case against the book, there was no case against the film. The danger was that the judge would find that there was more evidence to assess than could be dealt with in the week. We stressed to the judge the seventy actors and fifty crew who would lose their jobs and the financial loss we would suffer if the film was delayed. Luckily, he agreed and denied the injunction. We made our peace with Little Bird, agreed not to sue each other and not to impede the making of either project.

THE SHOOT

We started shooting at the courthouse in Lucan. There was still no reaction from the criminal fraternity. Ironically, Veronica Guerin was driving from the Lucan courthouse when she was shot in her car.

I had not made a film in Ireland since directing *Excalibur* in 1980 and producing Neil Jordan's *Angel* in 1982. I was surprised and impressed by the skills and professionalism of the crew. The many films made here over the last few years had honed their crafts. They combined great concentration with fine good humour, a difficult mix to maintain.

One day when we were shooting in the centre of Dublin, one of Cahill's sisters appeared and knocked on the door of Brendan's dressing-room. She spent an hour talking about her brother, how charismatic he was. Brendan said that all the social and political

xxi

Shooting

comment I had put in Martin's mouth (grinding my own axes) turned out to be uncannily accurate. As she left she added, 'Martin always said they would make a film of his life.'

I felt nervous about my own money being on the line, but relaxed about the shoot. Partly, this was because for the first time in my career I was answerable to no studio, no producer, no financier, for we still had no deal. Partly, it was because, since I lost my daughter Telsche to cancer, a year back, making a movie did not seem as vitally important as it once was. I had a little more perspective. Telsche worked with me a lot and she was the person who could always calm me down on the set when my temper flared. Her memory, her loss, was still keeping me on an even keel.

To get insurance cover, the director and the key actors are required to have medical check-ups. These are fairly perfunctory. They take your blood pressure, tap your chest and you tick off a list of diseases that have not afflicted you. But the insurers had second thoughts. They decided that I was integral to the film and that I could not be replaced, so although we were already shooting, they required me to submit to a more rigorous examination. The cardiologist informed me that the treadmill test indicated heart disease. I should check into the hospital right away. I might need bypass surgery; I could have a heart attack at any time. I said it was impossible for me to have surgery since I was shooting a movie, calling to mind Bill Stair's often-quoted remark about people taking film-making too earnestly: 'It's not a matter of life and death, it's much more serious than that.' And so much for my new philosophical, detached approach to the process. The specialist advised me against violent exercise. I went on a rigorous no-fat diet. This took the edge off the pleasure of the shoot. The film had found its voice by now. There was a synchronicity. Things clicked into place. We were at one.

Five weeks into an eleven-week shoot and the bank deal was at last on the verge of completion. We were borrowing money to keep the picture going. However, there was the matter of the insurance cover. I had failed the insurance medical. Kieran came through again. He simply never submitted the results for additional cover and whenever it came up for discussion, he managed to change the subject.

We finished the schedule with a week of nights. Our last night was in the Wicklow Mountains above Luggala. In *Excalibur*, I had Merlin striding across this very hill. It was magically still. The sky was clear and the stars bent low over our little endeavour. We spoke with the muted voices of interlopers in a cathedral. On such nights the spirits make their presence felt. We would not have been surprised had some ancient Celtic chieftain with the face of Martin Cahill appeared in our midst.

Some of the cast had finished early, at 10 p.m. and repaired to a pub in the nearby village of Roundwood. They bravely and selflessly kept on drinking in order to keep the pub open until our arrival at 3 a.m. At 7 a.m. I retired to my bed. The others decided that if they left then, they would catch the rush-hour traffic into Dublin and it would be wiser to wait until 11 a.m., which they did. The truth of it was, no one wanted it to end.

I took a flight to LA to see a top cardiologist. He examined me and pored over my stress test. He was perplexed. I was not overweight. I did not smoke. My cholesterol was normal. There was no history of heart disease in my family. The only way to be sure, he said, was to have an angiogram. A catheter was duly inserted into the artery at my groin and the long slim tube was pushed up to my heart. It squirted a dye into the system and I lay there and watched on a TV screen blood flowing and pulsing through my arteries, heart and valves, a more dramatic image than anything I had been able to achieve over the last eleven weeks. There no obstructions, no narrowing of the arteries – nothing!

'You don't have heart disease,' he told me, 'you probably never will. You will die of something else.'

I and my worried family were staying with my friend Bob Chartoff in Malibu. I got back from the hospital and watched the late sun back-lighting the big Pacific rollers. I was seeing everything intensely, as if for the first time. I had been on death row and the pardon arrived at the eleventh hour.

I went back to the relaxed pleasures of the editing room and Ron Davis and I shaped the picture. Richie Buckley and Van Morrison added the music. Everyone who came in to see the rough cut marvelled at Brendan's performance. Soon I would have to get out there into that tough market and offer my wares for sale. But not just yet.

John Boorman

The General

Fade in.

EXT. COWPER DOWN. DUBLIN. DAY

Leafy suburban street. Sunlit. Martin Cahill, the General, emerges from his house. His face is puffy. He walks unsteadily to his Renault 5.

Stops. Sniffs the air, sensing something amiss. Eerily deserted, except for a corporation worker at the end of the cul-de-sac ticking off passing cars on his clipboard. Cahill is under constant surveillance. Where are the police? Have they given up? Has he beaten them, finally? It seems so. He gets in the car.

He drives to the stop sign at the end of the street and halts. The man with the clipboard sprints across to the car. He produces a .357 silver-plated Magnum revolver from under his coat, aims. Cahill sees the face

of his assassin for an instant before the window shatters and the bullet crashes into his skull.

The car jerks forward, juddering its way across the junction, collides with a garden wall. Stalls.

The hitman runs to the car, pumps two more rounds through the window, leans in to make sure the General is dead.

An old man, walking the street, lowers himself to the ground and lies face down on the pavement. Faces appear at windows.

A child stares over the garden wall, not ten feet from the killer who looks up, grins.

His accomplice, disguised as a courier, roars up on a motorcycle. The hitman climbs on the back, still grinning. They ride off.

INT. SPECIAL SURVEILLANCE UNIT. DAY

A dozen young Gardai working at desks, lounging, talking on phones in a cramped office. They look up as the police radio crackles.

RADIO VOICE

Tango One is down! Tango One is down!

A roar goes up. Jubilation. They hug each other.

GARDA

They got the General.

EXT. COWPER DOWNS. DAY

Squad cars. Swarming with Gardai. Two women, Cahill's wife Frances and her sister, Tina, sob in each other's arms. His son, Tommy, arrives on a bicycle which he hurls at the police cordon.

TOMMY

You'se did this! That's me da. He's not dead, is he?

He fights his way through the cordon. A burly cop restrains him, pins his arms.

INT. SPECIAL SURVEILLANCE UNIT. DAY

*The door of an inner office opens and Detective Inspector Ned Kenny
enters the room. The young Gardai crowd around to congratulate him.
His stern look rebukes them.*

KENNY

This is no a victory for us.

EXT. COWPER DOWN. DAY

*Ned Kenny arrives at the murder scene. He is ushered through. A TV
Reporter thrusts a mike into his face.*

REPORTER

Inspector Kenny, the IRA are claiming responsibility. Do you
have any comment?

*Kenny shakes his head, passes through the cordon. A Young Detective
briefs him.*

YOUNG DETECTIVE

The press wants to know why was there no Gardai presence.
They're trying to suggest we were in collusion with the IRA.

*Kenny gives him a withering look. The body has been removed from the
car and covered in clear plastic. Kenny stares at the bloodied face. Close
on the features distorted by death and plastic. The noise and clamour die
on the soundtrack.*

EXT. COWPER DOWN. DAY

FLASHBACK: *the grinning face of the hitman. He has just fired the first
shot.*

*The shattered car window. The shot reverses. Time reverses. The shards
come together. Cahill looks up at his nemesis. His face morphs to the
twelve-year-old he once was. The boy looks up defiantly at the man who
will kill him thirty years hence.*

EXT. ALLEY. DAY. 1962

*Twelve-year-old Martin Cahill with two of his brothers. He is clutching
a loaf of bread and a bunch of cream buns. His brothers carry each end*

of a sack of potatoes. They are running flat-out down a long narrow alley. Sounds of pursuit.

EXT. HOLLYFIELD. DAY

They dodge into the warren of crumbling buildings. Appalling squalor. Rubble, refuse, broken windows, ragged kids everywhere. Two Gardai with a German shepherd on a leash are in pursuit. Several men and youths appear from doorways. They pick up stones and bottles and hurl them at the Gardai who are stopped in their tracks. They fend off the missiles.

INT. CAHILL FLAT. DAY

Martin and his brothers enter, panting and posturing. They dump the sack of potatoes in the centre of the one-room flat. Martin plants his boot on top of the sack like a conqueror. Several smaller siblings dance around the sack in delight. Their mother looks up wearily from the sink.

MRS CAHILL
You're shaming me, Martin.

Martin grins and pulls a packet of Sweet Afton from his pocket. He holds it out to her.

MARTIN
Will I take 'em back?

She laughs despite herself and reaches for the cigarettes. Martin snatches them back. She chases him round the room. He tosses them to her and stuffs a cream bun into his mouth. He runs out on to the balcony to watch the retreating Gardai.

EXT. BALCONY. DAY

The ten-year-old girl from next door, Frances, comes to his side and looks adoringly at him. Martin glances back to make sure his brothers are not watching then hands a cream bun to the girl. She hesitates to take it.

MARTIN
It's fresh, Frances. Only nicked it half an hour ago.

7

She sinks her teeth into it blissfully. He bites on his. They share a moment of swooning pleasure.

EXT. BUTCHER'S SHOP. NIGHT

The boy Martin carrying a skinned lamb on his back jumps over a wall into the arms of a patrolling Garda. He tries to wriggle free. The Garda punches him in the stomach. The boy doubles up and falls to the ground.

INT. CORRECTION SCHOOL. DORMITORY. NIGHT

A line of boys bending over the ends of their beds with their nightshirts hitched up. A priest beats the bare arses with a leather strap. Not every boy. One or two are passed over. The priest reaches Martin, hesitates, then moves on to the next. Martin is perplexed.

Later: Martin is sleeping. He wakes with a start. The same priest is groping under Martin's covers. He smiles at Martin, signals him to be quiet.

Martin punches him in the mouth. The priest slaps the boy's face with a stinging blow. Then another and another. Martin covers his head with his arms. The priest leaves.

Martin has a swollen eye and nose. He sits across a table from his mother. She has brought Frances with her. No one can think of anything to say. Martin sighs heavily. Close on Frances watching him.

> FRANCES
> (*accusingly*)
> You said you'd never get caught.

Fast pan to Martin.

> MARTIN
> I never will again.

Fast pan to Frances, now grown up. A similar room in an adult prison.

> FRANCES
> They're evicting us. All of us.

Fast pan to the adult Martin Cahill in prison clothes. He flares with anger.

> MARTIN
> No. They can't do that, Frances. We won't leave Hollyfield.
> No way do we go.

> FRANCES
> (*gently*)
> They're offering us a flat on Kevin Street.

He is enraged and struggles to keep his voice down. Frances glances nervously at the watching prison warder.

> MARTIN
> That's a deliberate insult to a criminal. Them flats is opposite
> the Garda station.

> FRANCES
> (*apologetically*)
> They're nice flats.

> MARTIN
> Nice! What's nice? Neighbours that'll lie for you. That's nice.
> A place where cops shite in their pants if they have to go

9

there. That's nice. Don't you understand, Frances. We're the dregs, the lowest of the low. That's why we stick together and help each other, because it's Us against Them. That's why we belong in Hollyfield.

Frances sniffs, not convinced.

FRANCES

Four little kids in one room.

MARTIN

But happy. Happy. Aren't our kids happy? Weren't we happy there as kids? No. I won't go. I'll drag them through the courts.

When we cut back we discover that Frances' place is now taken by Martin's slightly furtive solicitor, Lawrence Lawless.

LAWLESS

As your lawyer, Martin, I have to advise you against it. It will be expensive and you'll lose in the end.

MARTIN

I don't care what it costs. I pay you, don't I? I know youse charge me double what you ask civilians. You rob me without having to break into my house. You break in through the fucking letter-box.

INT. MOUNTJOY PRISON. DAY

Martin Cahill, not yet the General, steps into freedom: the prison door shuts behind him. He wears his 'uniform' of an anorak over a Mickey Mouse T-shirt and jeans.

EXT. HOLLYFIELD. DAY

The residents, mostly women and children, huddle in groups, watching resentfully as corporation workers dump their furniture and belongings out in the street. Dozens of Gardai armed with riot shields and batons enforce the eviction. Kenny is talking to a group of women as Noel Curley, Martin's lifelong friend, is ejected from his flat.

KENNY

The children will be better off. You won't know yourself
there. Lovely park, schools, everything.

NOEL

(*to Kenny*)

You're behind this, Kenny. We'll deal with you, you're a big
man now with your boys behind you.

KENNY

I'll have you anytime, Noel Curley, one to one, you scumbag.

*Martin, carrying his suitcase, breaks into a run as he sees what is
happening. He finds Frances and the four children. Her younger sister,
Tina, is helping her. The kids jump into his arms. He hugs them, tears
flow.*

MARTIN

Yer da's here. We're not going anywhere. We're staying.

He looks up at the men carrying out the furniture.

They better not touch any of our stuff.

Frances reassures him.

FRANCES

They haven't, Martin.

Kenny is walking towards Martin.

Don't lose yer rag, Martin. Don't give him the satisfaction.

KENNY

Martin, you mad whoor. Frances, it'll be nice to get out of
this sewage and filth.

FRANCES

Don't touch my kids.

KENNY

Martin come over here.

They walk off.

You're a clever fella. You're not like these thugs. You have a cleverness; that's a responsibility. Do you want your kids to grow up with your troubles? Get out of this cesspitt. Get a job.

> MARTIN
>
> Sergeant Kenny do you think I could get a job in the police? Going around throwing women and children out on the street, fucking people out of their homes.

> KENNY
>
> Martin.

> MARTIN
>
> I'd love that, you know. Smashing up the kip. You better not touch any of my stuff, and you're not putting me out of here either. My appeal's pending. Frances, let's go home. The law is on my side.

She gathers the children and hurries to his side. Tina joins them. They walk to the desolate block of flats.

> KENNY
>
> Stay in the gutter if you're happy there. Stay there.

INT. HOLLYFIELD BUILDINGS. DAY

Men with sledgehammers smash up the squalid flats.

EXT. HOLLYFIELD. DAY

Demolition proceeds. Cahill's corner flat is still standing. He has erected a flagpole from which flies the Tricolour. Two huge loudspeakers on the roof blast out 'Que Sera Sera'. Incongruously, his gleaming Harley Davidson sits outside. Dust and debris everywhere. Frances and Tina clamber over the rubble to get to the door.

INT. CAHILL FLAT. DAY

Martin sits in front of a big colour TV watching a video and eating a cream bun. Frances coughs from the dust as she comes in. Tina picks up a suitcase.

FRANCES

I'm begging yer, Martin. On me hands and knees.

She kneels before him. He takes her in his arms.

MARTIN

I can't, Frances. I got me principles.

FRANCES

Principles? You're loving it.

Tina kisses him on the cheek.

TINA

Selfish bastard. My sister's too good for you.

He smacks her bottom. She squeals.

EXT. HOLLYFIELD. DAY

Martin roars up on his Harley. They have flattened his home in his absence. Corporation officials watch his reaction nervously from a distance. He grins and waves at them.

Jump cut. A caravan is parked on the site of Cahill's flat, the flag still flying. The Harley stands next to it. The door opens. Martin comes out into the sunlight, yawning and stretching. He is wearing pyjama bottoms and a Mickey Mouse T-shirt.

MARTIN

What can I do for youse gents?

Ned Kenny with two Gardai flank a pompous Corporation Official and a Priest.

OFFICIAL

On the failure of your appeal, I have to inform you, Mr Cahill, that if you do not vacate this site in forty-eight hours, you will be forcibly removed.

MARTIN

And I have to inform youse that I'm having you lot up before the European Court of Human Rights.

He begins to warm to his task.

You dumped us in here when it suited you. Now you think
you can sling us out when you feel like it.

The Priest steps forward.

PRIEST

Martin, I know the hardships suffered in this parish.

MARTIN

Fuck off, the lot of you. Yer're all oppressors a the poor. Civil
fucking servants. Garda fucking Sichona. Parish fucking
priests. Get the fuck out a me house.

EXT. DETACHED HOUSE. NIGHT

Martin climbs down a drainpipe with a bulging duffel bag on his back.

EXT. HOLLYFIELD. NIGHT

*With the duffel bag still across his back, Martin rides home on the
Harley from his night's work. He stops and watches his caravan
consumed by flames.*

EXT. HOLLYFIELD. DAY

The wreck of the caravan has been dragged to one side, a tent erected in its place. The flap opens and Martin peeks out blearily.

MARTIN

Why do you fucks always call in the afternoon? You know I'se a night-worker.

He is confronted by an impressive delegation headed by the Chairman of the Housing Committee.

CHAIRMAN

Martin, I'm the Chairman of the Housing Committee and I've come myself to ask you to back down quietly so we can start building much needed houses on this site.

Although half his face is hidden by the tent flap, the other half is twinkling with amusement.

MARTIN

Well, Chairman. I won't go to Kevin Street. Give me a flat in Rathmines and I'll fold me tent.

CHAIRMAN

Wouldn't you sooner live closer to your own kind?

MARTIN

No. I want to live closer to me work. All the big houses.
(*laughs*)
Only kidding.

The Chairman and company laugh uneasily.

EXT. SWANN GROVE. DUSK

Martin leaves for work carrying a sports bag. Frances and Tina see him off proudly from their new home. The kids swarm at their feet. Martin gives them a wave and a fond smile. He pulls on his balaclava.

EXT. DUBLIN SIDE STREET. NIGHT

Martin, balaclava-clad, holds a gun to a Security Man's head and walks him to the back of his truck. The Security Man opens the door. There are several sacks inside. Martin and his four accomplices are speechless as Martin opens a sack.

It is full of ten-pence coins.

> MARTIN

What the fuck?

> SECURITY MAN

From the gas meters.

EXT. DUBLIN MOUNTAINS. NIGHT

Martin, his two brothers, Anthony and Paddy, and two close associates, Willy Byrne and Noel Curley, are now revealed without their balaclavas. They stagger from their van, each with a sack of coins on his back. The ground is boggy and gouged out from turf-cutting. There are pyramids of turf drying. Anthony's foot sinks in and he topples, cursing, into slushy water.

Martin piles turf around the sacks to conceal them.

INT. POOL HALL. NIGHT

Only one table is illuminated. It is covered with ten-pence coins. They have turned green from the damp. Martin, Paddy, Willy and Noel are cleaning them with Silvo. They have pints of Guinness perched on the table rim, cigarettes hanging from their mouths, all except Martin who neither drinks nor smokes. Through the half-open door to a back room, Anthony can be seen on a bed with a girl.

> NOEL

No disrespect to your judgement, Martin, but was that the best place to hide them?

> MARTIN

Shut the fuck up and keep rubbing.

> PADDY

Jaysus. This is worse than working.

MARTIN
(*shouts*)
Anthony! Get finished in there. Come and help us launder this money.

They go on smoking and drinking and polishing.

Paddy, I want you to watch that house tonight.

PADDY
It's lashing rain, Martin. We've cased it for two weeks. It's a fucking tomb. Yer man's in Hong Kong.

MARTIN
Any deliveries, Willy?

WILLY
Not a thing. I been there three days on the trot.

MARTIN
All day?

WILLY
Yeah. Told youse.

MARTIN
Right. We'll take it tonight.

PADDY
Don't think I can come. Elbow's fucked.

He rubs it ruefully. Anthony wanders in from the back room pulling on a joint. Martin snatches it from his mouth and tosses it away.

ANTHONY
(*enraged*)
If you weren't my brother.

MARTIN
You're no good to me with your brain fried. And youse.
(*turns on the others*)
No more stout till we get back.

EXT. FITZGERALD HOUSE. NIGHT

Martin and his four men pull up outside a large house in a suburb of Dublin. A light comes on inside and Martin throws a sharp look at Willy.

> WILLY
> Comes on every night. It's on a timer.

They pull on their balaclavas and get out of the car.

INT. FITZGERALD HOUSE. NIGHT

The men crawl in through a small window at the side of the house. They find themselves in the drawing-room.

The light comes on. A man wearing a tuxedo stands before them with his hand on the switch. His name is Fitz Fitzgerald, a property developer. A frozen moment of mutual astonishment.

> WILLY
> Who the fuck are you?

> MARTIN
> Who the fuck you think he is.

Martin clouts Willy on the side of the head with his revolver.

> In Hong Kong, is he?
> (*to Fitz*)
> Get up against the wall.

Martin and the others dash through the house while Anthony trains his sawn-off shotgun on Fitz.

INT. KITCHEN. NIGHT

Martin surprises a Chef and his assistant cooking dinner.

Their arms shoot up when they see the gun waving at them.

> MARTIN
> Out.

> CHEF
> Can I take the sauce off the flame, or it'll spoil?

Martin sniffs at the saucepan. Dips his finger in. Tastes it. It's good. He looks around, finds a loaf of cut white bread, grabs a slice, soaks it in the sauce and stuffs it in his mouth. The sauce leaves a brown rim around the mouth of the woollen balaclava.

The Chef winces as Martin drives them out of the kitchen and the sauce boils over.

INT. DRAWING-ROOM. NIGHT

Martin shoves the cooks into the room.

> MARTIN

Lie down.

They do. He turns his attention to Fitz.

Why you got up like the dog's fucking dinner?

> FITZ

I always dress for dinner.

> MARTIN

Don't give me that bollocks. Your da was a culshie builder from Leitrim. Came here and fucked up Dublin.

Willy comes in.

> WILLY

Can't find the safe.

> MARTIN
> (*to Fitz*)

Where is it?

> FITZ

There is no safe. And there's nothing of value in the house. My wife left me three months ago and she took everything worth taking.

> MARTIN

Robbed by yer own wife? The competition we face today. Everyone's at it.

As the thieves crease up with laughter, the doorbell sounds. Panic. Martin dashes to the window.

INT./EXT. FITZGERALD HOUSE. NIGHT

A man in tuxedo and a woman in a long dress wait at the door.

INT. DRAWING-ROOM. NIGHT

Martin throws a questioning look at Fitz. He shrugs.

>   FITZ
> Dinner guests.

Martin and Willy go to the front door.

INT./EXT. HALLWAY. NIGHT

Martin opens the door and yanks the man inside. Willy pulls the woman in. At gun point the couple are driven towards the drawing-room.

A number of jump cuts as five more couples arrive. The same routine. Door pulled open. Startled faces. Shoved down the hallway.

INT. DRAWING-ROOM. NIGHT

The Chef, his assistant, and six couples are lying in neat rows on the floor. Noel and Anthony have been collecting money and jewellery in a bowl. Anthony totals up the take and hands it to Martin.

>   ANTHONY
> Unbelievable. Thirty-five quid between all them whoores.

>   NOEL
> A definite shortage of liquid assets, boss.

Martin takes out a jeweller's eye-glass and examines the rings and broaches, tossing aside in disgust the ones of little value, which seems to be most of the haul. Anthony, Willy and Noel are swigging beer from bottles through the wool of their balaclavas. There is white froth where their mouths should be.

There's money here somewhere. I can smell it. The place
stinks of it. Take his pants down.

*Martin wrenches the flex from a lighted lamp. Anthony holds Fitz in an
arm lock while Willy pulls down his pants and underpants. Martin
gives the flex to Willy.*

See if this'll jog your memory.

FITZ
If there was a safe, I'd tell you. I'm insured. It wouldn't be a
loss for me.

MARTIN
You're a fucking liar.

*The guests on the floor dare to murmur dissent: Why do you need to
humiliate him? He's a decent man. Can't you see he's telling the truth?*

Martin turns on them in fury.

Decent? He's a worse criminal than any of us. When he sold
that building in Fenick Square to the state, he made three
million profit in three months. Three million! That's a pound
for every man, woman and child in this fucking country.

*He warms to the task, ranting and waving his arms. The captives
watch his gun nervously as he bangs it down for emphasis. He turns on
Fitz.*

You took a quid off every little kid. Babes in arms. Kids with
no boots. Kids with no arse in their pants. You fuck.

FITZ
For God's sake. It was just business.

MARTIN
Business? Who's the fucking robber here? We're amateurs
compared to him. Give him one of those short, sharp shocks
they're always talking about giving us.

*Willy jabs the wires at Fitz's testicles. Anthony lets go of Fitz's arm and
leaps back yelling. He kicks Willy in the head.*

22

ANTHONY

YOU GOT ME, YOU PRICK.

Later, Fitz and his guests are still recumbent. The room has been ransacked. The thieves are raging with frustration. Martin is eating profiteroles while quizzing the men.

MARTIN

What you got?

MAN 1

Range Rover.

MARTIN

You?

MAN 2

BMW.

MARTIN

You?

MAN 3

Ferrari.

MARTIN

Give us the keys. I'll have that.

ANTHONY

You can't drive that yoke round town.

MARTIN

I got to get some pleasure out of the night.

He strides out. The others follow, shouting threats and carrying a few worthless souvenirs.

EXT. RATHMINES. GARDA STATION. NIGHT

Martin roars up in a Ferrari and skids to a halt. He leaves a note on the windscreen, sounds the horn and strides off into the darkness.

A Garda comes out into the street. He looks up and down the street, then notices the Ferrari with its engine running. He walks over and takes the message from the windscreen. It reads: 'CHECK THE OWNER. A PADDY WITH A FERRARI HAS GOT TO BE A CROOK.'

INT. SWANN GROVE FLAT. NIGHT

Frances and Tina are feeding the four children. Martin watches TV.

FRANCES

You want something, Martin?

MARTIN

I'll eat out tonight. Anything you want?

He gets up, pulls on his coat and stuffs his balaclava into a pocket.

TINA

See if you can find a train set for Orla, there's a dote.

INT. CRENSHAW HOUSE. KITCHEN. NIGHT

Martin stands, illuminated by the light of the fridge. He chews on a lamb chop, drops the bone on the floor, takes another, closes the door. He moves off stealthily.

INT. STUDY. NIGHT

Martin's flashlight probes the walls and comes to rest on a golden disc in a frame. The inscription reads: 'TO BRIAN CRENSHAW TO CELEBRATE THE SALE OF 1,000,000 COPIES OF BLUE SMOKE LOVER.' Martin slips it into his bag.

INT. NURSERY. NIGHT

A revolving night-light splays moving shadows on the walls. Two children sleeping. Martin runs his flashlight over the lavish collection of toys. He stops on a train.

EXT. UPPER HALLWAY. NIGHT

Martin moves silently and slowly down the hallway. The door of the master bedroom opens. Martin presses himself into an alcove. A man in pyjamas emerges. He looks back at his sleeping wife then moves silently down the corridor and enters a room at the far end. Martin carefully opens the bedroom door and stands watching for a moment then enters.

INT. BEDROOM. NIGHT

He goes to the bedside and regards the sleeping woman. He picks up a box of pills and reads the prescription by the shaded light of his torch. He shakes her shoulder gently. She does not stir. He takes the Cartier watch from her bedside table, wanders to a bureau and scoops up some jewels. On the vacant side of the bed he finds a wallet and removes the money. His swag bag is bulging.

INT. UPPER HALLWAY. NIGHT

Martin opens a door a crack and watches the husband screwing the nanny.

INT. SWANN GROVE FLAT. NIGHT

The four children sleep in a double bed that fills the tiny room. Martin places the train on the end of the bed.

He goes into the other bedroom, which is not much bigger. Frances and Tina are asleep. Tina's left breast is exposed. Martin stands stock still admiring the curve and swell of it.

He slides into bed next to Frances and curls into her naked back. Tina flings out an arm in her sleep and it rests on Frances' shoulder. Her hand is inches from Martin's face. He brushes it with his lips as he begins to rub against Frances. She wakes with a gasp as he enters her. He puts his hand over her mouth to guard against further noise. Slowly and silently they make love. His eyes are fixed on Tina's sleeping face.

INT. SWANN GROVE FLAT. DAY

Martin is tucking in to a big fry-up at the kitchen table. His wife and sister-in-law sit across from him. They have cooked up a plan and they glance nervously at each other as they try to sell it to Martin.

> MARTIN
>
> If I own a house, the tax people will get after me. And I'll lose me dole money.

> FRANCES
>
> Put it in Tina's name. We can move there with the kids and she can live here. She needs her own place.

> MARTIN
>
> Is that what you want, Tina?

> TINA
>
> It'll still be the same. You can come over here when you want to get away from the kids. And I'll help Frances over there.

Tina pours him more tea. Frances piles his plate from the frying pan. He looks into their pleading and loving faces.

> FRANCES
>
> And you can have your own pigeon loft like you always wanted.

> MARTIN
>
> How much they want?

> FRANCES
>
> Eighty grand.

Martin winces.

> It's a lovely house, Martin.

MARTIN
(*sighs*)
I'll go round me hiding places tomorrow. See what I can scrape up.

They hug and kiss him. He struggles to get a forkful of food between their faces and into his mouth.

Frances pulls away and frowns as she remembers a snag. Tina bounces on his lap like a child.

FRANCES
There's just one thing, Martin. They won't take cash.

Martin flares with anger. He snaps:

MARTIN
Jaysus. What's this country coming to? They don't trust paper money any more?

He struggles to his feet, sliding Tina away. He picks up the gold record which he has removed from its frame. He is working himself into a rage.

Everything's fake today. Look at this. Gold record? Sprayed with gold paint is all.

He contemptuously snaps the vinyl in half.

INT. BANK. DAY

Martin walks into the busy bank shielding his face with his hand. He dumps a duffel bag on the counter.

MARTIN
I want a banker's draft. There's eighty grand in there.

Close on fingers counting notes.

Martin watches two clerks complete the check. The bank manager has appeared and watches sternly. He looks hard at Martin.

MARTIN
Good day at the races.

Close up of bankers draft for £80,000.

27

EXT. BANK. DAY

Martin exits the bank, slipping the draft into his pocket. He crosses the street to a Garda station. Before entering he turns and makes a discreet hand signal. Anthony Cahill and Noel Curley, standing outside the bank, acknowledge the signal.

INT. GARDA STATION. DAY

Martin goes to the desk.

MARTIN

I want to see Detective Sergeant Kenny.

GARDA

Inspector Kenny.

MARTIN

Oh, promotion.

GARDA

Name?

MARTIN

Martin Cahill.

The Garda is startled. He lifts the phone.

INT. BANK. DAY

Anthony and Noel, wearing motorcycle helmets to conceal their faces, go to the counter where the two clerks are still sorting Martin's cash.

ANTHONY

I'd like to make a withdrawal.

NOEL

What you got there? Looks about eighty grand. That'll do.

Noel whips out a Magnum revolver and jabs it at the clerk's head.

INT. GARDA STATION. DAY

Ned Kenny comes to the desk.

KENNY

What do you want, Cahill? Come to confess a few crimes?

Martin gives him a sweet smile.

MARTIN

Just wanted to welcome you to the neighbourhood, Inspector. It's nice and peaceful after Hollyfield, isn't it?

KENNY

You know why they sent me here, don't you, Martin?

MARTIN

Not because of me, I hope.

KENNY

Yes, because of you. Because they think I know your wiles and ways, and I do. It's only gonna end one way, you know, Martin, if you keep on like this.

INT. BANK. DAY

Anthony reaches across the counter and scoops the money into a duffel

29

bag. They stride out of the bank, Noel pointing the gun over his shoulder.

INT. GARDA STATION. DAY

Martin is lounging against the counter. Kenny fixes him with a hard look, but Martin won't meet his gaze.

> KENNY
> I'm a poor bloke, I got nothing, debts up to here, but I can sleep at night, you see.

> MARTIN
> I seen you outside my flat a few times. Come in for a jar next time you're passing. Have a chat.

An alarm sounds. A Garda runs out from an inner office.

> GARDA
> Bank robbery! Across the street!

Kenny glares at Martin. He gets it. Martin shrugs.

> MARTIN
> Disgraceful the profits these banks are making.

> KENNY
> You made a right bollix of me. Congratulations.

Kenny runs out with the other Gardai.

INT. COWPER DOWN HOUSE. DAY

A four-bedroom detached house in a pleasant suburb. Martin and Frances stroll through the empty rooms. She is alight with excitement. He is morose.

> FRANCES
> Isn't it lovely, Martin?

> MARTIN
> We don't belong here. You want to be like the whoores who live in this street?

FRANCES

We never will. It's still Us against Them.

*They have wandered to the front bow window. There is a police car
parked outside. The two Gardai are staring in at them.*

MARTIN

Better get some curtains.

*He turns away and they walk into the back. They watch Tina playing
with the children in the big back garden.*

Why doesn't she get a fella?

FRANCES

She says, where am I going to find someone like Martin.
(*she laughs*)
She's half in love with you.

MARTIN

Yeah. Well.

EXT./INT. VIDEO GAMES ARCADE. DAY

*Close on a padlock. A pair of long-handled metal clippers shear off the
padlock which secures the steel-mesh curtain leading into the arcade.*

*Martin and Noel, in full motorbike crash helmets, roll up the steel
curtain.*

*They burst in and head for the pay kiosk where a large, tough-looking
woman is counting the previous night's take.*

Arcade woman presses panic button.

*Close on Martin as his helmet scrapes against the metal grille of the
kiosk.*

*Noel has an automatic pistol which he points at the woman. She shrugs
and without a word hands them a pile of bank notes. Lined up on her
table are dozens of bags of silver coins. Martin piles them into a sack
which he produces from under his coat. When it is full he finds it is too
heavy to lift. Noel takes one end and they stagger out with it.*

31

EXT. STREETS. DAY

They heft the bag up on to the pillion seat of their motorbike. Martin drives and Noel gets on behind with the money bag wedged between them.

Martin drives off. As he turns the corner, he sees a Garda patrol car coming towards him. He turns the bike and accelerates away. The patrol car puts on its siren and flashing light.

Taking corners fast, changing direction often, the bike outpaces the patrol car but to Martin's disgust the chase is joined by a police motorcycle which sticks to his tail.

INT. GARDA CONTROL ROOM. DAY

Ned Kenny stands before the big wall map of Dublin. He calls over to the radio operator.

> KENNY
> Tell the Garda to keep a distance. They're armed and we are not.

EXT. STREET. DAY

The Motorcycle Garda hears the instruction crackle under his helmet.

> MOTORCYCLE GARDA
> Roger. Turning into Antrim Street, heading north.

INT. GARDA CONTROL ROOM. DAY

Kenny studies the map.

> KENNY
> Get a car to block the top of Capel Road.

EXT. STREET. DAY

Martin makes a fast left then a right turn. He curses as the Garda motorbike reappears in his mirror. He calls back to Noel.

> MARTIN
> Throw the bag on to the road.

NOEL

Why?

MARTIN

Just do it. Do it when I swing into the middle of the road.

Noel heaves the heavy bag over the side. The coins burst out from the sack and cascade over the road.

The Garda on the motorbike swerves to avoid them but they get under his wheels and the bike skids out from under him.

Noel is jubilant. Martin twists and turns in and out of side streets then brakes to a skidding stop.

EXT. ALLEY. DAY

Abandoning the bike, they hurry down an alley. They throw their weapons over a wall. Martin stuffs the bank notes under a dustbin.

A police car screeches to a stop at the end of the alley. They turn back and start running.

The Garda on his motorbike appears at the other end. He rides towards them.

INT. GARDA INTERVIEW ROOM. DAY

Ned Kenny sits across from Martin Cahill.

KENNY

We've got the bike, the weapons, the money. Armed robbery. You're looking at twelve years, Martin. For what, for pennies?

Martin stares at the wall. He shows no reaction.

MARTIN

I don't want to talk to youse men.

KENNY

Your kids will be teenagers. Think of that. You'll never see them growing up.

MARTIN

I don't want to talk to youse men. I don't want to talk to
youse men. I don't want to talk to youse men.

*Martin chants it like a mantra, his eyes fixed on the same point on the
wall.*

INT. FORENSIC LAB. DAY

*Dr James Donovan examines the evidence gathered against Martin and
Noel: the motorbike, the bank notes, the silver coins, the bag that held
them, the clothes they wore, the weapons.*

INT. INTERVIEW ROOM. DAY

Lawrence Lawless is now present.

LAWLESS

My client informs me that he was walking quietly in the street
when he was brutally assaulted by Gardai. You have no
witness to connect him to this crime. I insist you release him
immediately.

KENNY

You've had your reasonable access and we have the evidence.
Door!

The cell door is opened and Lawless is shown out.

INT. GARDA INTERVIEW ROOM. DAY

*Kenny and Martin are alone again. Kenny allows himself a wolfish
grin. He leans close to Cahill.*

KENNY

Cast your mind back, Cahill.

INT. FORENSIC LAB. DAY

*Donovan picks at Cahill's motorcycle helmet with a scalpel, removing
the faintest smudge of paint.*

FLASHBACK: *Martin's helmet brushing against the metal grille in the
video arcade.*

34

KENNY
(*voice-over*)
Remember that slight collision in the arcade, Martin? With the fucking helmet.

Donovan examines a tiny shred of leather through a microscope then slides Noel's glove under it.

FLASHBACK: *Noel's hand gripping the steel-mesh security screen in the arcade.*

You left a trail of evidence a mile long.

Pincers remove blue fluff from the bag which held the silver coins.

FLASHBACK: *The money bag rubbing against Noel's donkey jacket as he rides on the pillion of the motorbike.*

Careless. Amateur.

INT. SWANN GROVE. NIGHT

The small living-room is jammed and smoke-filled. Martin has gathered his gang together – Willy Byrne, Noel Curley, his brother Paddy and several others. Tina comes in with a tray of beers and gathers up the empties. Martin follows her with his eyes while he talks.

MARTIN
All them cheap stick-ups, creepers and mooching. It's demeaning. Before I go down for a long stretch, I want to do a big one, something to really embarrass the Gardai.

WILLY
Why bother, Martin. You're the best at what you do.

MARTIN
I got caught. When I'm inside I'll have to admit I was sent down for stealing ten-pee fucking coins. It's humiliating.

PADDY
You're a creeper. It's your nature. You'll never give up creepin'.

A lot of raucous laughter. Martin grins.

MARTIN

It'll always be me hobby.

Tina looks in to see if anything is needed. She smiles at Martin.

Besides. I got a family to support. So has Noel. They'll need a
lot a money if I go down for twelve. Paddy's got a sentence
hanging over him too. So, this is what we're going to do.

He pauses dramatically. They fall silent. He lowers his voice.

We're going to do O'Connor's. There's two million in gold
and jewels in there, and it's ours.

*Whistles and gasps. Greed and fear are generated in equally large
amounts.*

NOEL

It doesn't matter to me. I'll be going down with you, Martin,
so getting nicked for another job won't make much difference
but the IRA cased O'Connor's and even with their fire-power
they gave up on it. That's a fucking fortress.

Martin smiles and calls out.

MARTIN

Come on in.

*A man enters into the room from the passage. He has a hood tied over
his head.*

TINA

Why's he wearing that in here?

MARTIN

Go and lie down for a bit, Tina.

*Tina leaves, feeling humiliated. Martin, enjoying the drama, puts an
arm around the hooded man in a fond fashion.*

You don't need to know this bollix and he doesn't need to
know you whoores. He works at O'Connor's and he's kindly
offered to help us out.

The assembled criminals are suitably impressed.

If word of this plan gets out, I will know who done it and he will die. Youse all know the rules.

INT. COWPER DOWN HOUSE. DAY

A birthday party for one of the kids. Noel and his wife are there with some of their offspring. Frances and Tina are fussing with the food. The young boys have toy guns and are enjoying a shoot-out. Martin shows the kids his pigeons in the newly constructed loft.

Later: Martin and Noel are chatting. Tina comes over with one of Martin's beloved cream cakes and pushes it into his face. She runs off but he grabs her and pulls her to him. She tries to squirm away, but he holds her head between his hands and kisses her on the mouth, transferring half the cream cake to her.

She collapses on the floor in a heap of giggles. Frances watches ruefully. She comes over with a cloth and gently wipes Martin's face. He goes back to Noel.

> NOEL
> It's going to be hard, leaving them all. Criminals shouldn't have families. Makes us soft.

Martin's face hardens.

> MARTIN
> Fuck 'em. I'm not going to let them put me away this time.

> NOEL
> This is a hard rap to beat.

> MARTIN
> That woman can't identify us. Not with the helmets on. It's the fecking forensic bollix. That bastard Donovan.

EXT. SUBURBAN STREET. DAY

Dr Donovan gets into his car, starts the engine. The car explodes. Donovan opens the door and drags himself out as flames engulf the interior. His leg is mangled. He passes out.

INT. CRIMINAL COURT. DAY

Martin sits with his head in his hands. He is flanked by Lawless and his counsel, Henry Mackie. Noel and his counsel are alongside.

The State Prosecutor, Arthur Ryan, is addressing the court.

> **RYAN**
> I beg the indulgence of the court in asking for an adjournment. I am assured that Dr Donovan will recover and is determined to testify.

The Judge casts a stern eye on Martin and thunders his judgement.

> **JUDGE**
> The perpetrator of this heinous crime will be hunted down and brought to justice. If this wicked person happens to be in this court let me remind him that sentences for perverting the course of justice are some of the most severe that this court can inflict.

Martin looks up with an innocent 'Who? Me?' expression on his face. Noel, on the other hand, looks decidedly shaky.

INT. POLICE CELL. NIGHT

Kenny is sitting across from Martin who stares at the wall showing no emotion. Sergeant Higgins, tough and burly, is at his shoulder looming over him.

> **MARTIN**
> I don't want to talk to youse.

> **KENNY**
> I don't want to talk to you, you scumbag. We know the type of bomb.

> **MARTIN**
> I don't want to talk to youse.

> **KENNY**
> So, you had to get it from the paramilitaries, probably a renegade. The IRA won't like this. They'll start their own inquiries. The Provos. You know what that means. Next time

your door gets kicked in, you'll be fucking praying it's the police.

MARTIN

I don't want to talk to youse.

KENNY

You talk to him then.

Kenny nods to Higgins to take over and leaves.

HIGGINS

Then let's talk your own language.

He kicks Martin in the kidneys. Martin doesn't flinch or react. Higgins kicks him again.

MARTIN

Higgins has a black dog. Higgins has a black dog.

Higgins thumps Martin in the gut. Once, twice, three times.

HIGGINS

You touch my dog I'll kill you.

He rains down punches until Cahill slumps unconscious.

INT. POOL HALL. NIGHT

It is late at night. All the tables are lit and many of them have scattered balls on the green baize as though in mid-game. A group of men waits. They fall silent as Martin appears. Slightly bent, he limps over to a table. They are in awe of him now.

A map and other plans are spread out under the light of the pool table. Martin, now very much the General, is planning the assault on O'Connor's. Paddy and Anthony are missing. There are a couple of new faces.

MARTIN

I want to know when they crap, where they go for a wank and a doze. We've got to know more about those security men than their mothers would ever want to know.

WILLY

They drink at Paddy Murphy's pub before going on duty.

MARTIN

Then you be there every night, Willy.

He peers at a rough sketch of the alarm system.

This is from our man inside. Not good enough. Jimmy, I want you to break into the alarm company, Hensons, who fitted this system, and nick the plans.

EXT. O'CONNOR'S. NIGHT

Martin (still limping) and Noel Curley walk along the perimeter of the tall wall that surrounds the factory. Martin looks up at the coiled barbed wire on top of the wall.

NOEL

Electrified.

They turn the corner. A Garda patrol car pulls up outside the main gates. A Garda gets out, checks the gate, speaks to a security man on the inside.

MARTIN

How often does that happen?

NOEL

Off and on all night.

EXT. O'CONNOR'S. DAY

Martin and Noel watch the entrance from a parked van. There is a double gate for vehicles and a pedestrian door next to it. Martin looks at his watch: 7.55 a.m. A man waves at the camera and the door opens automatically.

MARTIN

The manager?

NOEL

On the dot. Every morning. They disarm the alarm between them. They each have half the code.

40

> MARTIN
Ah, now. This is their weak point.

> NOEL
But look.

The workers begin to arrive. They line up to punch in and are checked by the security men as they enter one by one.

> MARTIN
How many?

> NOEL
Just over the hundred.

> MARTIN
Now that's a bit of a bollix.

EXT. FOUR COURTS. DAY

Martin sits in a parked car across the street watching the crowd of press and television reporters awaiting the arrival of Dr Donovan.

His car pulls up and he is helped out by Gardai. Using crutches he makes his way slowly up the steps towards the courts. Spontaneous applause breaks out.

Martin turns to an accomplice in the back seat.

                              MARTIN
    Off you go, Jimmy.

Jimmy pulls a balaclava over his face and gets out. He wears Martin's standard Mickey Mouse T-shirt and anorak.

He crosses the street and is immediately mobbed by the press. They hurl questions at him: 'Do you deny responsibility for blowing up Dr Donovan?' 'Show your face!'

Jimmy pushes his way through them but is finally hemmed in. He stops. More cries of 'Show your face!' Dramatically, he pulls off the balaclava. Martin watches the charade from the edge of the crowd. He grins then strolls towards the courts unseen.

                              JIMMY
    What seems to be the problem here?

The press people howl their frustration and run towards the courts. Some of them catch a glimpse of Martin as he enters the court.

INT. COURT. DAY

The court stands as the Judge takes his seat. Kenny has his eyes fastened on Martin who lounges in his place, hands covering his face like a bored child in the classroom.

The woman from the video arcade awaits her call. She looks as bored as Martin.

                              JUDGE
Before the adjournment several members of the jury complained of being followed and their homes watched. For the remainder of this trial I order the jury to be sequestered in a hotel under the armed protection of the Gardai.

Martin leans over to Noel and whispers behind his hand.

                    MARTIN
Jaysus. I'm running out of ideas.

Arthur Ryan, gets to his feet.

                     RYAN
I call Dr James Donovan.

As Donovan limps painfully to the witness stand, applause again breaks out from the public gallery.

INT. POOL HALL. NIGHT

Martin has his motley team standing in a line on one side of the lit pool table. He paces on the other side. The table is strewn with maps and papers.

                    MARTIN
First.

                    HARRY
I nick a car on the North Side.

                    MARTIN
Shea?

                     SHEA
I take one in Terenure.

                    MARTIN
When?

                HARRY AND SHEA
Ten p.m.

                    MARTIN
What kind of motor?

                    HARRY
Nothing flash. Reliable.

                    MARTIN
The van?

                     GARY
Got it in me garage already. Tuned up.

MARTIN

What we wearing?

GAY

We're a soccer team. Sweats and trainers. Burn them after.

MARTIN

And?

GAY

Er. We wear our own clothes under.

MARTIN

What do you have in yer bags?

NOEL

Equipment.

MARTIN

And any gun that's fired?

GARY

We get rid of it.

MARTIN

Get your alibis rock solid. And remember, don't trust a
woman to lie for yer if you're cheating on her.

SHEA

What about your alibi, Martin?

MARTIN

If I can keep me case going, mine's perfect. The heist, a
course, will be out of hours. But when they come looking for
us, I'll be in court.

*There is an air of expectation, repressed excitement, new-found
discipline. A sentry darts into the room and gives a shrill warning
whistle. The gang scatters to the tables. They pick up cues and start
potting balls. Two Gardai walk in and survey the innocent scene.
Martin pairs off with Gary.*

GARY

Will it be tomorrow, Martin?

MARTIN

I'll let you know, Gary.

He puts his arm around Gary.

I want you to pull a little stroke for me in court tomorrow.

INT. COURT. DAY

Dr Donovan is giving his evidence. Photographs are handed to the members of the jury together with chemical analysis reports.

DONOVAN

You will see that the analysis confirms that the paint on the helmet is identical to that on the grille in the arcade.

Gary stands up in the public gallery and calls out.

GARY

Martin Cahill is a murderer and a drug dealer. He deserves to be sent down for life.

Gardai run to seize Gary who flees from the court. The Judge calls for order. When the rumpus subsides he addresses Martin's counsel.

JUDGE

I will not tolerate this kind of outrage, Mr Mackie.

MACKIE

I'm as outraged as you, Your Honour. However, my client claims no knowledge of this man and I must point out that the accusations made just now could influence the jury against my client and I ask you to declare a mistrial.

JUDGE

Members of the jury, this is a cynical ruse and I direct you to disregard what was said.

He turns his attention back to Martin and his counsel.

Are you taking up a study of the law, Mr Cahill? Continue, Dr Donovan.

INT. LAW LIBRARY. NIGHT

Martin squeezes through a window and drops down next to a sign which announces 'TRINITY LAW LIBRARY'.

Close on a legal tome. Martin's finger tracing the words which are illuminated by his flashlight. The section is on armed robbery – Section 23 of the Larceny Act 1916.

Martin at a library table. Several books are open. He looks up, grinning. He punches the air.

INT. TERRACE HOUSE. NIGHT

Martin squeezes through another window.

He creeps up the stairs to a landing. He opens a door. An old Woman sleeps in the bed. Martin closes the door.

He opens another door, smiles. The Woman from the arcade. She is snoring.

Martin goes to her bed-side and gently shakes her shoulder. She wakes with a start, alarm in her eyes. He puts his finger to his lips, ssh. He whispers to her.

                          MARTIN
See, I been doing a bit a reading tonight, yer know? And it seems that if you were not in fear of yer life, like, when we took the money from yer, then they can't do me.

                          WOMAN
Jesus. What?

Martin shows her the gun.

                          MARTIN
Now if you say in court that you *were* in fear of yer life, I'll make sure that you *are* in fear of yer life. Got that?

EXT. O'CONNOR'S. NIGHT

Martin, sitting in his car, shoots at a street lamp with a .22 rifle. Noel is with him.

Two men are high up on a cherry-picker purporting to mend the lamp next to the electrified wall.

Martin puts out cones to block the road, makes sure there is no traffic.

He looks back at the cherry-picker, gives an arm signal.

The cherry-picker driver turns out to be Willy. He swings the cradle jerkily closer to the building. Noel prises open the window.

INT. POOL HALL. DAWN

It is not much of a soccer team, what with the pot bellies and cigarettes, but the dress and sports bags are convincing. Martin wishes them luck and they troop out into the Dublin night.

EXT. O'CONNOR'S. GATES. DAY

Martin sits in one of the stolen cars. He consults his watch: just coming up to 7.55 a.m. He raises his hand and looks in the rear-view mirror.

Gary in the van is parked close behind him. Gary acknowledges the signal and starts the engine.

The manager appears. He walks to the side door and waves up at the security camera.

INT. O'CONNOR'S. COURTYARD. DAY

The security man opens the door and the manager enters. They go together to a wall panel and disarm the alarm system.

Noel and Gay in balaclavas appear, guns pointing at the two men.

While Gay covers them, Noel runs to the main gates and quickly unlocks the many bolts.

EXT. O'CONNOR'S. DAY

Martin checks his watch: 7.56. The gates open. Gary's van roars inside. The doors close instantly.

> MARTIN
> Go, Jimmy. You're on.

Jimmy has been crouching in the back of the car. He springs up, gets out and sprints across the road. He is wearing the uniform of a security guard. He stands at the side door of the factory.

INT. O'CONNOR'S. COURTYARD. DAY

Gary and the others leap out of the van and head inside the building.

INT. LIFT. DAY

Gay drives the manager and security man into the lift where the other three guards are already incarcerated.

EXT. O'CONNOR'S. DAY

The workers are arriving. Jimmy stands at the gate.

> JIMMY
> They've got a problem with the alarm. Only be a few minutes.

WOMAN

You're new, aren't you?

JIMMY

Yeah. My first night. Just my luck.

The workers pass the word back to the new arrivals. They light up cigarettes and gossip. They look up at the sound of a dull thud from within.

Across the street in the car, Martin looks at his watch: 8 a.m. He speaks into a walkie-talkie.

MARTIN

Is the shop open? Over.

NOEL
(voice-over; coughing)

Looks good.

INT. SAFE ROOM. DAY

It is full of smoke, but the huge safe door is open. The gang swarms inside. They whoop with joy at the sight of stacks of gold bars and trays of jewels.

EXT. COURTYARD. O'CONNOR'S. DAY

Loading the van. Men lurching under the weight of gold. Running back and forth.

EXT. O'CONNOR'S. DAY

The hundred workers, mostly women, mill about. Jimmy is still explaining.

A Garda patrol car drives up, slows at the sight of the crowd.

Martin twitches as he watches. He speaks into the walkie-talkie.

MARTIN

Hold on. Don't come out.

INT. O'CONNOR'S. COURTYARD. DAY

The last man scrambles into the back seat and slams the door. The van is already moving towards the gates. Noel, about to open them, holds up his hand to Gary as he gets Martin's message.

Tense faces of the men in the van as they crouch on their crock of gold.

EXT. O'CONNOR'S. DAY

The Gardai peer out of their patrol car. Jimmy gives them a reassuring wave. They drive on.

Martin watches them go. Then, into the walkie-talkie:

MARTIN

Now.

The gates swing open. The van roars out, scattering the crowd. Martin's engine is running. He starts off. Jimmy runs across the road. Martin reaches across and opens the passenger door. Jimmy and Noel jump in. They speed off in the opposite direction from the van.

EXT. WASTE GROUND. DAY

The van screams to a stop. The vacant lot is shielded by tall factory walls on three sides.

The men leap out of the van and begin tearing off their sports clothes and put on regular clothes from their bags.

Martin drives up with Jimmy. They discard their track suits and throw them into the car.

The others set fire to the two cars and walk off, scattering in all directions.

INT. VAN. DAY

Martin, Gary and Noel turn into a back alley and drive into the open doors of a repair garage.

INT. GARAGE. DAY

They open the back door of the van and stand in awed silence, staring at the gold glowing dully in the half-light.

Martin breaks the spell. He takes a neatly folded pile of canvas bags and hands them to the other two.

MARTIN

Here. Divide up. Everyone gets the same.

They start with the gold bars, one in each sack, then another.

GARY

You're the General. You should get more than us.

MARTIN

I will, because when youse have pissed yours against the wall, stuck it in yer arm and up yer nose, I'll still have mine.

They work quickly and methodically to fill the bags.

Later: the work is completed. Martin goes to his Harley which is parked in the garage alongside the van.

MARTIN

Noel and I have to go. You wait, Gary. The bags'll be picked up and hidden safe.

                        GARY
    Where?

                       MARTIN
    Better you don't know.

Noel opens the garage door. Martin starts the bike.

                        GARY
    One a them's mine. I got a right to know.

                       MARTIN
    You don't have the right to live unless I say so.

He looks at his watch.

    Get on, Noel. We're late.

Noel gets on the back and they ride off.

EXT. CRIMINAL COURT. DAY

Martin parks the bike. He and Noel hurry towards the court.

                       MARTIN
    Where's the press today? All down at O'Connor's, I suppose.

                        NOEL
    You left the key in.

                       MARTIN
    What bollix is going to steal my bike?

INT. COURT. DAY

*Martin and Noel slip into their places just as the Judge takes his seat.
Martin raises his hand. He is enjoying himself and cannot resist making
mischief.*

                       MARTIN
    Yer Honour. Could we finish early today so I can draw me
    dole?

*Later: the Woman from the arcade is on the stand being questioned by
Ryan.*

RYAN

So, afraid for your life, you handed over the money?

MACKIE

Objection. Leading the witness.

JUDGE

Sustained.

RYAN

I'll rephrase that. With this gun pointing at your head, why did you give them the money?

Ryan smirks and there are titters around the court.

WOMAN

Well, wouldn't you?

RYAN

So you were afraid you would be shot?

WOMAN

Not really. I'm used to it. It's happened a few times. They never shoot.

RYAN

But they would if you did not give them the money?

WOMAN

I don't know. I always give it to them.

RYAN

But surely a terrifying experience.

WOMAN

I wouldn't say that.

Martin nudges his counsel with his elbow. Mackie gets to his feet.

MACKIE

Your Honour, I refer to Section 23 of the Larceny Act 1916. If the State cannot show that the victim was in fear of her life, the charge cannot be sustained and I call for an acquittal.

EXT. COURT. DAY

Later: great jubilation as several of Martin's gang members congratulate him on his acquittal. Newspapers are thrust into their hands. They devour the headlines gleefully: 'BIGGEST ROBBERY IN THE HISTORY OF THE STATE', *and so on.*

Kenny and Higgins watch, furious with frustration. As Martin passes Kenny he waves the newspaper headlines at him.

MARTIN

You should be out catching the big criminals instead of bothering us little fellas.

He leaves with his phalanx of admirers.

HIGGINS

We'll take you down, Cahill.

INT. LIBRARY. NIGHT

Beavis, the fence, is sitting at a desk, examining the trays of jewels. He

makes notes about each stone. Martin stands at his shoulder. The
members of the gang are seated at desks or sprawled on top of them.

Beavis makes some calculations.

> BEAVIS
> There's roughly a thousand carets of diamonds and three
> thousand carets of rubies and sapphires and sundries. The
> whole lot is worth around one million pounds.

He pauses and they wait attentively.

> My offer is fifty thousand pounds for the lot.

Angry cries. Everyone is talking at once. Martin holds up his hand.

> MARTIN
> The least we'll take is ten per cent of its value. We're not
> going to haggle. It's beneath us. So if you want to leave here
> alive . . .

He laughs. They all laugh. He's kidding, isn't he? Beavis joins in. He
raises his hand in submission.

> Mr Beavis has also made an offer for your gold. Twenty
> thousand pounds per man.

> BEAVIS
> That's delivered to me in London, of course.

That is his safe conduct guaranteed.

> MARTIN
> Don't leave yer cigarette butts lying around. We might want
> to use this place again.

EXT. CAHILL PIGEON LOFT. DAY

Jimmy (he who dressed up as a security man) is holding a bird, stroking
it, displaying it to Martin.

> JIMMY
> She's got stamina. She's brave. She has pedigree. She's a
> winner.

What are you asking?

JIMMY

A lot a money, Martin. But you can have her for what I paid.
I won't take a profit. Not from you.

Martin nods thoughtfully. He has a deeper agenda.

MARTIN

How often do you take the ferry, Jimmy? With the pigeons.
Flying them or buying them.

JIMMY

Every couple a weeks. At least.

EXT. JIMMY'S YARD. NIGHT

*A secluded place which cannot be overlooked. A big pigeon loft. Boxes,
cages and junk everywhere. Antique furniture lying around, dubiously
acquired.*

*Jimmy and Martin have removed the door panels of Jimmy's purpose-
built pigeon van and are secreting gold bars.*

EXT. DUBLIN – LIVERPOOL FERRY. DAY

*Jimmy is in a line of cars embarking. He is waved down by a harbour
policeman. His knuckles are white on the steering-wheel. The pigeons
coo in their cages behind him.*

He rolls down his window. The Security Man looks inside.

SECURITY MAN

Where's the race from this week?

JIMMY

Milton Keynes . . . I don't know if it's a poet or a place.

SECURITY MAN
(*laughs*)

Good luck, now.

Jimmy is waved through.

EXT. MILTON KEYNES. DAY

Jimmy consults his watch, pulls a lever. A hundred tiny doors open on the side of the pigeon van and, with a roar of wings, the birds soar into the sky.

EXT. COWPER DOWN HOUSE. DAY

Close on Martin squinting up at a hot grey sky. A wide shot looking down at the back garden reveals Tommy, Orla, Sylvie and Patrick gathered around their father, craning their faces to the sky, searching the heavens. Tina and Frances come out from the house, shading their eyes, looking up.

Martin looks anxiously at his watch.

A pigeon appears in the sky, weary but flying bravely.

Martin sees it. His face lights up. He points. The children cheer.

Martin hurries up to the loft. He beams with pride as the pigeon flutters into the loft.

INT. PIGEON LOFT. DAY

Martin catches the pigeon, takes its marker and enters it in his racing clock.

EXT. GARDEN. DAY

Looking down – a pigeon's-eye view – as Martin runs back down into the garden, whooping with delight. He scampers around in circles pursued by the kids then falls to the ground. The children pile on top of him.

INT. POOL HALL. NIGHT

Noel and Gary escort Jimmy into Martin's presence. Something is wrong and Jimmy is decidedly nervous. A little queue of supplicants is filing past Martin. He hands out money and cans of food from cartons stacked up next to his seat.

JIMMY
Heard about your brother, Anthony. Sorry for your troubles.

57

MARTIN

Yeah. Died in jail.

JIMMY

Was it the warders? Brutality was it?

MARTIN

No. It was the smack. Which you have a liking for too, Jimmy, and you addicts are always short a money.

JIMMY

I got it under control.

Martin nods to Willy and he shepherds out the remaining people. Jimmy watches them go.

Half them bollix is having you on, Martin. Lying bastards.

MARTIN

It's my way of paying taxes.

Without warning, Martin slaps him hard across the face.

You're a gold bar short on that last run. Where the fuck is it?

JIMMY

Martin, I never would. On me mother's life.

MARTIN

So, did it grow legs and run away?

JIMMY

Honest.

MARTIN

Own up and I'll let you off with a knee-hammering.

Jimmy shakes his head. Martin nods to the other two. They grab Jimmy and wrestle him to a pool table. Noel takes one arm, Gary the other. They hold each hand down on the wooden rim of the table.

Martin produces a hammer and a couple of four inch-nails.

I'm goin' to nail this problem down once and for all so it don't come back to haunt me.

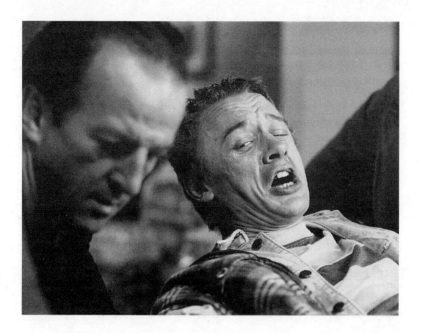

He puts the point of a nail in the upturned palm and raises the hammer.

JIMMY

I swear. I never took it. I'd tell yer if I knew.

MARTIN

You're a fecking liar. Only for the pigeons I shouldn't a let you join in the first place.

He raises the hammer.

JIMMY

Jaysus Christ.

MARTIN

Yeah. You'll soon know how He felt. Talk.

JIMMY

I dunno. I dunno.

The hammer comes down.

EXT. POOL HALL. NIGHT

Shea, on guard outside, winces as the cry of agony reaches him.

INT. POOL HALL. NIGHT

Martin is sitting in the corner of the room eating a cream cake. He stares thoughtfully at Jimmy, both of whose hands are nailed to the table. He moans softly, semi-conscious.

Martin, making a decision, gets to his feet.

> MARTIN
> The bollix is innocent. No one could take that much pain without talking.

He takes a pair of pliers from his bag.

INT. EMERGENCY ROOM. HOSPITAL. NIGHT

Martin leads a very groggy Jimmy into the emergency room. His hands have been roughly bandaged with Martin's Mickey Mouse T-shirt.

> MARTIN
> You come through with flying colours, Jimmy. I'll see you never want. You're me man.

Jimmy nods his assent. Martin looks around as nurses and doctors pass back and forth without acknowledging them. He bellows out.

> Come here, one of youse. There's a man hurtin' here.

EXT. DUBLIN STREET. DAY

Martin and Noel stride up to a busy street corner. They stop and search the faces of the people crossing back and forth. Two severe-looking Men approach them. They are senior officers of the Provisional IRA.

> MARTIN
> So, what you want with me? I been up all night dealing with one of me own men.

> IRA MAN
> Yeah. The crucifixion. It's the talk on the street.

Martin shakes his head, appalled. Nothing is private any more.

Congratulations on the O'Connor job.

> MARTIN
>
> Yeah. It was too tough for the IRA, I hear.

He grins, enjoying his superiority. No smiles from the IRA Men who keep a wary eye on passers-by.

> IRA MAN
>
> You're getting into drug dealing.

> MARTIN
>
> Not me. Don't hold with it.

> IRA MAN
>
> Some of your men are buying up heroin. Now they're flush with money.

> MARTIN
>
> That's up to them. We've all got our hobbies. I'm into pigeons, meself.

IRA MAN

You can let them know the IRA will take measures against them.

A very pregnant pause.

MARTIN

Is that all you wanted? You could have sent me a postcard.

The IRA Man moves closer to Martin and speaks into his ear. Martin recoils from the intimacy.

IRA MAN

We want half the O'Connor haul.

Martin steps away, waving his arms and shouting.

MARTIN

If you want gold, rob yer own gold.

IRA MAN

Keep your voice down.

Martin pays no heed. He storms off, Noel following nervously in his wake. He calls back at the IRA Men.

MARTIN

You do your strokes and we'll do ours. Yer not getting a fucking penny, you dossers. There's nothing as low as robbing a robber.

Noel tugs at him.

NOEL

Go back. Play them along. Why aggravate them?

Martin will have none of it. Noel turns and gives a shrug and a wave to the IRA Men.

INT. COWPER DOWN HOUSE. NIGHT

Martin stands morosely at the window staring into space. Frances is ironing clothes.

FRANCES

What's the matter with you? Walk away, why don't you.

MARTIN

I got a lot on me mind. I got the IRA on me back. I hurt
Jimmy when I shouldn't have. Half me men are drug addicts.
It's a bollix.

Frances sits down beside him.

FRANCES

You're a good man, Martin. How many husbands don't drink
or smoke or run around with other women?

She is struggling to control her feelings. She turns away from him.

Why don't you go round the flat and see Tina. We've had a
talk, me and her. I don't mind. Keep it in the family.

The prospect does not lift his mood. He still looks morose.

MARTIN

Yeah. I've been thinking about it.

Frances cuddles up to him.

FRANCES

I'm glad that's settled.

63

INT. SWANN GROVE FLAT. DAY

*Martin is eating a hearty breakfast in the kitchen. Tina, in a cotton
dressing-gown, is pacing, talking in the wall phone. She is very aware of
Martin's eyes as he looks back and forth from her to his eggs and bacon.
There is a languid sensuality about her movements. She giggles into the
phone and turns shyly away from Martin.*

                    TINA
    Yes, he did . . . that too . . .

Martin protests.

                    MARTIN
    Enough, you two. Tell Frances to come over here instead of
    talking behind me back.

*Tina ignores him. Something Frances says makes her helpless with
laughter. Martin turns his attention back to his food.*

EXT. EMPLOYMENT EXCHANGE. DAY

Martin, smiling, eating a cream cake, strolls into the dole queue.

*Noel catches up with him as he enters the building. He looks worried
and is out of breath.*

Martin shuffles forward. Noel whispers in his ear.

                    NOEL
    They've taken Gary. Lifted him off the street in broad
    daylight.

                    MARTIN
    The IRA?

                    NOEL
    For pushing drugs.

                    MARTIN
    Was he?

                    NOEL
    Well, not pushing. Buying and selling. You know, ducking
    and weaving is all. But they're naming all of us, even those

64

who don't go near drugs. They're whipping the people up against us. It's mayhem.

MARTIN

Let me get the dole money then we'll see what can be done.

Noel dashes off. Martin waits patiently in line. He started to sing quietly to himself.

EXT. CRUMLIN ESTATE. DAY

As Martin approaches Noel's house he sees it is under siege from a mob. They brandish banners proclaiming: CONCERNED PARENTS AGAINST DRUGS.

Stones are thrown. Windows broken.

Martin keeps a distance. He pulls out his mobile phone and dials.

Noel opens the door and faces his accusers. The Leader of the CPAD is standing in front.

CPAD LEADER

You're destroying our kids wid yer drugs. We're throwin' you
out a here.

*There is a roar of approval as Martin speaks on the phone. He puts a
hand over his ear against the noise.*

MARTIN

Twenty-eight, Anders Road, the Crumlin. Yeah, you can hear
them. Course not. You Gardai, you're never around when
you're needed.

*Noel is on his doorstep, struggling to be heard. He wards off a Coke can
aimed at his head.*

NOEL

You people know me. I'm not a pusher. I'm not a user.
Which one of youse has ever seen me selling drugs? Come on.
Which of you?

CPAD LEADER

We all know what you are, Noel Curley. A fucking crook
who'd stoop to anything. You got two days to get out of
here.

*The crowd cheers its approval. Martin prowls around the edges of the
demonstration.*

*The two IRA Men are watching the affray. Martin is almost on top of
them before he spots them. Before they see him, he turns his back on
them and joins the crowd in shouting abuse at Noel.*

*Police sirens. Gardai spill out and insert themselves between Noel and
the angry crowd.*

INT. POOL HALL. NIGHT

All the members of the gang are there and a few new faces.

*Martin makes a dramatic entrance. Gary has a leg strapped and his
jaw is wired up. His face is badly bruised.*

Gary tells me what they were really after was where the
O'Connor loot was stashed. This anti-drug shit is just a
smokescreen.

Gary tries to speak. Martin leans down to catch the garbled words.

He says they threatened to nail his hands to the floor.
(*he grins*)
Well, imitation is the sincerest form of flattery.

*They always laugh at Martin's cracks and this is no exception. Jimmy
waves his still-bandaged hands to show that he can take a joke. Martin
raises a hand for quiet.*

Now, all a youse. Stay away from the drugs. This is a battle a
wits. We got to let the people know that we're ordinary
decent criminals not dealers and pushers. The IRA is trying
to turn the people against us. Our own people.

*He pauses, surveys the faces. He loves the drama, the control he has
over them.*

They're going after Noel tomorrow. They want to toss him
out of his house. We'll be ready for them.

EXT. CRUMLIN. DAY

*With their banners flying, the Concerned Parents Against Drugs march
down the street towards Noel's house . . .*

*Marching towards them is the bizarre spectacle of a hundred and more
men, most of them in balaclavas, with banners held high reading:*
CONCERNED CRIMINALS AGAINST DRUGS. Martin is tucked in at
the back.

*As they come face to face, men from the CPAD come forward swinging
pickaxe handles and iron bars. The two IRA Men can be glimpsed
behind them.*

*Two criminals in the front reveal weapons. Stand off. Noel steps
forward.*

NOEL

You know who the real pushers are. Go after them. But don't
try and molest ordinary decent criminals.

CPAD LEADER

You know who they are too. Why don't you go after them if
you're that concerned?

NOEL

Just get away from my house.

*There is a dangerous moment, then some of the CPAD turn away, then
others, and finally the rally breaks up. Martin comes up to Noel.*

MARTIN

Good. Now we can get back to business. I've had an idea. Do
you know anything about art?

*Noel is still pumped up from the confrontation. He looks askance at
Martin.*

NOEL

Art? No. Do you?

MARTIN

I don't know anything about art but I know what I like . . . to
steal.

INT. RUSSBOROUGH HOUSE. DAY.

*Close up of a Vermeer painting of a woman writing a letter. Her maid
stands at a window behind her. Martin studies it with an intensity not
unlike love.*

*A Guide is taking a group around the collection. There are four nuns,
three aged ladies and Martin, Frances and Tina who is heavily
pregnant.*

GUIDE

Apart from one owned by the Queen of England, this is the
only Vermeer in private hands. It was one of the paintings
stolen by the IRA in 1974 and thankfully recovered. It would
probably fetch in excess of twenty million pounds on the open

market. Sir Alfred Beit has announced his intention of gifting it to the National Museum.

Martin consults his guide book and puts a circle around the Vermeer. He has also marked up two by Rubens, a Gainsborough and a Goya.

FRANCES
How does anyone get the kind of money that buys all this?

Martin's attention has moved from the paintings to the alarm system. He studies the position of the infrared sensors on the panelled walls.

MARTIN
This Alfred Beit's got some hole in the ground in South Africa that's full a diamonds. He pays blackies about two pound a week to dig 'em up for him. I seen it on the telly. He has them x-rayed every day when they clock off to make sure they haven't swallowed one.

Frances peers at the Vermeer.

FRANCES
What's she writing?

TINA

Gotta be a love letter.

Martin looks back at the picture.

MARTIN

Shopping list. Maid's waiting to go down to the corner shop.

Same location. Another occasion. Different crowd.

Martin is with Gary and Noel. They stroll through in an over-casual way. Gary, still bruised and limping, looks at a voluptuous Rubens nude. He nudges Noel.

GARY

Look at the knockers on that one.

Noel ignores him. The enterprise is making him very nervous.

NOEL

Who's going to fence paintings for you, Martin? There's plenty of other good stuff here.

I've made me mind up.

Noel shrugs, knows how stubborn he is. Martin is staring intently at the Vermeer. Gary squints at it, perplexed.

GARY

Twenty mil for that bollix? I can't see it.

Martin looks at him disdainfully.

MARTIN

It's class. You wouldn't know about that, Gary.

Gary turns away, snubbed. He eyes up two Japanese girls.

GARY

I tell you what is class – the fucking security system. Armed Gardai here in ten.

Martin, still looking dreamily at the painting.

MARTIN

I got it worked out.

The other two look nervously at the General.

EXT. GROUNDS OF RUSSBOROUGH. NIGHT

Martin, Noel, Gary, Shea and Willy are crouched behind bushes watching the great eighteenth-century stately home. They are all dressed in navy-blue denim overalls and cotton gloves.

MARTIN

Now!

Gary and Shea pick up a lightweight ladder. They run to a window. Noel inserts a blade and opens the window lock. The alarm goes off, an ear-splitting clanging. Noel lifts the big Georgian window and they all clamber inside.

INT. PAINTING GALLERY. NIGHT

Martin lights his flashlight which guides him to the door. He turns on the light.

Gary shins up the ladder. He inserts a piece of chewing-gum to cover the infrared light sensor. Shea carefully cuts the wire on the window contact.

They jump back out of the window.

EXT. RUSSBOROUGH. NIGHT

Noel inserts his blade and relocks the catch. The whole operation takes less than two minutes. They run back to the thick bushes.

Their faces: waiting, watching.

Police cars race in. Armed Gardai surround the house, which is suddenly blazing with light. Voices. Figures moving in the rooms, checking the paintings.

Martin tuned to the police radio, listens on an ear-phone. He repeats what he hears.

MARTIN
Nothing stolen. False alarm. They're leaving.

He gives a thumbs up. Grins and clenched fist salutes.

The police cars drive away. The lights in the house go out.

The gang moves stealthily to the house. Noel unlatches the window. They climb through.

INT. PAINTING GALLERY. NIGHT

They freeze for a moment, tense. Will the alarm go off? It doesn't. Relief.

Martin takes out his booklet and walks around like a tourist pointing to the paintings he wants. They lift them off the wall and stack them by the window. Martin hesitates by the Vermeer. He stares at it intently.

NOEL
Martin!

Martin snaps out of his reverie. He takes the Vermeer off the wall.

They climb out of the window and race across the lawn.

73

EXT. DEMESNE WALL. NIGHT

They throw the paintings over the wall, one at a time. Willy and Shea catch them on the other side. Two four-wheel drives are waiting for them. Martin keeps the Vermeer till last.

> MARTIN
> Don't drop this fucker.

He throws it. It has a heavy frame. Shea takes it on the chest and falls backwards. Willy dives to save it as it topples over. He just gets his hands under it.

Martin's face appears over the wall.

> Good lad, Willy.

They stash the paintings into the jeeps and drive off at high speed.

INT. JEEP. NIGHT

Willy is driving. Martin leans into the windscreen, peering out, looking for the spot. He signals Willy to slow down.

> MARTIN
> That's not it. Go on. Go on.

Willy jams his foot down and the jeep screams down the narrow unlit mountain road.

> Stop! Back up.

Willy throws it in reverse. They slam into the following jeep. They all leap out.

EXT. WICKLOW MOUNTAINS. NIGHT

Cussing and swearing. Noel berates Willy, pointing to the damage on the front of his jeep.

> WILLY
> What you worried about? They're not our cars.

> MARTIN
> Shut up. All of you. Get the paintings out.

They lug them out on to the side of the road.

Right. Willy. Gary. Off you go now.

They don't move. What us? Why?

Go on. Piss off. You won't know where they are, so you won't get blamed if they're nicked.

Reluctantly, they get into one of the jeeps and drive off. Noel and Martin lug the paintings across boggy ground into a copse of trees.

EXT. COPSE. NIGHT

Martin hunts around with his flashlight until he finds a hole covered with leaves. He brushes them aside and pulls back a rock. A cavern has been dug out and lined with plastic sheeting. They slide in the paintings.

Pushing the rock back in place. Tidying the leaves.

NOEL
Sure you'll know it again?

MARTIN
I got this well marked. Haven't I been up here breaking me back digging the fucker?

NOEL
We never found that fine silver you buried up here somewhere.

EXT. RATHMINES. GARDA STATION. NIGHT

Martin pulls up outside the station. He gets out. Noel slides over into the driver's seat.

MARTIN
They won't find the paintings are missing till morning. This'll be me alibi. You go on home.

Martin enters the station.

INT. RATHMINES. GARDA STATION. NIGHT

The night duty Garda looks up as Martin enters. They are well used to his visits now.

GARDA
What do you want this time, Cahill?

MARTIN
I'm making a complaint. Police brutality. I want to see
Inspector Kenny.

GARDA
He won't be here till morning.

MARTIN
I'll wait.

GARDA
All night?

MARTIN
Yeah.

GARDA
You pulling another stroke?

Martin sits on the hard wooden bench and stares at the wall. The wall stares blankly back at him. The ghost of the Vermeer superimposes on the institutional beige paint. The woman writes. The maid waits. Martin stares.

DISSOLVE TO:

Martin is asleep, stretched out on the bench. He opens his eyes and looks up. Inspector Kenny is staring down at him and continues walking towards his office. Martin gets up and follows him.

> KENNY
>
> Did you sleep well, Martin?

> MARTIN
>
> I can sleep at night.

They walk towards Kenny's office.

> KENNY
>
> I have to take my hat off to you now, do I? You're the General, is it? You're up there now amongst the famous criminals. You'll be in the record books.

> MARTIN
>
> What?

INT. KENNY'S OFFICE. DAY

They enter the office.

> KENNY
>
> Now you're an art connoisseur. You think there are buyers for this kind of stuff? If anyone does come after it, you'll never know if it's a sting or not. Maybe that'll be the end of you.

> MARTIN
>
> What have I done? I been here all night. I'm making a complaint.

Kenny sighs. He gets up, goes to his window, turning his back on Martin.

> KENNY
>
> I hear O'Connor's had to close down. A hundred people lost

their jobs. Ordinary decent people. Because of you. Man of the people.

MARTIN

They can go on the dole, like I have to.

Kenny turns to face him.

KENNY

You scumbag. I've been asking for a team to keep you under twenty-four-hour surveillance. They wouldn't give me the funds. Now with this, they will. We'll be all over you. You won't take a piss without us knowing about it.

(*looks at his watch*)

Seven-forty-five. You got your alibi, that's what you came for. Now get the fuck out of here, you prick.

EXT. DUBLIN STREET. DAY

Martin is on his way to collect his dole as usual. Two Gardai follow a few steps behind. A TV crew comes up alongside. The Reporter tries to

interview him on the hoof. Martin has a hood pulled tight over his face.
He keeps his hand up to disguise his features.

> REPORTER
> How do you feel about the Gardai following you everywhere?

Martin replies in a genial tone.

> MARTIN
> I never see them. I never see them. Seriously, I don't notice
> them at all. I have no interest in the police.

> REPORTER
> Do you deny you are Martin Cahill, the crime boss known as
> the General?

> MARTIN
> There must be another Martin Cahill.

He keeps walking towards the employment office. The Reporter stays on
his heels.

INT. COWPER DOWN HOUSE. NIGHT

Martin sits between Frances and Tina watching the impromptu
interview on television. Tina is heavily pregnant.

> REPORTER
> (*TV screen*)
> Who do you think the General is?

> MARTIN
> (*TV screen*)
> I dunno. Some army officer?

> REPORTER
> Why have the Gardai circulated notices about Martin Cahill,
> known as the General, wanted for armed robbery?

> MARTIN
> There's an Inspector Kenny. He's always trying to blacken
> me.

> REPORTER
> What do you know about the Beit paintings?

Martin furrows his brow in mock innocence. He stops just before joining the dole queue.

MARTIN

Not much. They were old yokes, weren't they? Done by a Dutch fella and a Spaniard. Isn't that right?

Frances looks proudly at Martin. The narrator continues describing Cahill's alleged exploits.

FRANCES

You come over ever so well, Martin.

MARTIN

Is that set adjusted right? Makes me look fat.

TINA

Not fat. Cuddly. Couldn't see your face though.

MARTIN

I was covering up, wasn't I?

On the TV is a shot of Gary being pursued by the Reporter. He turns, shouting obscenities which are bleeped out.

Gary turns on the Reporter and slugs him. Then he goes for the camera and his fist comes smashing into the lens.

EXT. COWPER DOWN HOUSE. DAY

Early morning. Martin leaves the house carrying a small tote bag. Two Gardai stand at the garden gate. They see Martin approaching but turn their backs, blocking his exit. Martin skips over the low wall and heads for his car.

GARDA I

Hey, Cahill. Which sister did you screw last night? Both?

Martin gets into his car, a modest Renault 5, without response. The Gardai get into their car which is parked right behind.

Martin drives off. The Gardai follow.

Martin stops at the end of the street. Noel is waiting on the corner. A Garda stands next to him, breathing down his neck. Noel gets into Martin's car.

INT. CAR. DAY

Noel looks very shaky.

> NOEL
>
> They're crawling all over us, Martin. My nerves can't take it.

> MARTIN
>
> Ignore them. They can't keep it up. They've got ninety men tied up watching us.

> NOEL
>
> Why'd you send for me?

> MARTIN
>
> We've got to take care of those paintings.

> NOEL
>
> Yeah. How?

He looks nervously over his shoulder at the following police car.

> MARTIN
>
> We'll shake them off.

> NOEL
>
> You don't have the pace in this.

Martin laughs.

EXT. WICKLOW MOUNTAINS. DUSK

The two cars are dots as they wind over the deserted moorland roads.

INT. CAR. DUSK

Martin checks his rear-view mirror. The police car is tight on their tail. Martin keeps to a steady forty miles per hour. Noel peers at the mileage on the dash.

> NOEL
>
> That's three hundred miles we've done. We should run out of petrol any minute now.

The tote bag is open on the seat. Frances has prepared them a nice picnic and they both munch on sandwiches.

MARTIN
Sooner the better.

EXT. MOUNTAINS. DUSK

Both cars have their lights on. They pass mounds of cut turf but there is not a soul or a house or another car in sight.

Martin's engine splutters then cuts out. The car slows to a stop. He gets out, goes to the boot, opens it, takes out a five-gallon drum and refills his tank.

INT. CAR. NIGHT

Martin gets back in and starts up.

MARTIN
Now we wait for them to run out.

EXT. MOUNTAINS. NIGHT

The police car slows to a stop. Martin's car drives away. He toots his horn.

INT. CAR. NIGHT

Martin strains to recognize the spot. There it is. He turns the car off the road into the shelter of a copse of trees.

EXT. COPSE. NIGHT

Martin's flashlight beam finds the hiding place. He scoops the leaves away and pulls back the stone.

He pulls out the paintings one by one and hands them to Noel.

Martin kneels down and turns his flashlight on to the Vermeer. Inside the frame, where the picture should be, is completely blank. Martin throws a vicious, accusing look at Noel.

MARTIN
Someone's whipped the fucking picture. Now what fucker would do that?

Noel and Martin peer at it more closely. A coat of grey mildew covers the canvas.

> NOEL

It's mildew, Martin.

Martin rubs it with the sleeve of his rough denim jacket. Part of the picture reappears. It is the Vermeer – the woman writing a letter. Martin grins with delight.

> MARTIN

Ah, Jaysus. There it is. She's still at the writing.

Martin peers fondly at the painting. Noel is getting edgy.

> NOEL

It won't take them long to catch up with us, Martin.

Martin gets to his feet.

They cut the canvases out of the frames, roll them up and seal them in plastic bags which Martin has brought in the tote bag. They work feverishly, on the edge of panic. Martin steps back and puts his foot through one of the paintings. He hops about trying to shake it off.

> MARTIN

Get this fucking thing off me.

He wrenches it off.

EXT. COWPER DOWN HOUSE. NIGHT

Martin gets out of his car. Several Gardai get out of two police cars and converge on Martin. The burly Detective Sergeant Higgins greets Martin at his gate with a grin.

> HIGGINS

That was a clever old stunt you pulled there all right, Martin. Chalk that one up, but by God, when you do fall, you'll fall heavy.

Martin goes past them without a glance. Higgins sticks his foot out as Martin passes and sends him sprawling on the garden path. Laughs and cheers from the Gardai. Martin gets up and grins at Higgins.

MARTIN

You're a great sportsman, Higgins. Aren't you the golf champion? It was you fought to get a private golf course just for the Gardai. No crooks allowed in. Only crooked cops. Well, you won't have any problem getting a hole-in-one in future.

EXT. POLICE GOLF COURSE. DAY

Higgins stands on the edge of a green shedding tears of rage. Deep holes have been gouged out. He roars.

HIGGINS

The bastard. The fucking bastard.

EXT. COWPER DOWN HOUSE. DAY

A traffic jam in the residential street. As each member of Martin's gang arrives, he is followed by a police car. Closely watched and photographed, Willy, Noel, Shea, Gary, Jimmy are admitted in turn.

INT. COWPER DOWN HOUSE. DAY

They are nervous and angry. Martin tries to calm them.

MARTIN

Treat it like a game and don't let them get to ya. All they want to do is wind you up so ya do something stupid and they'll nick yer for it or shoot yer.

Gary is clearly drunk. He stands up, waving his arms.

GARY

We can't pull no strokes with them watching. They'll starve us out.

MARTIN

Look at you, Gary. Legless and not even dinner time.

GARY

Fuck it. I can't face it without a drink. And me jaw still hurts.

They all start talking at once. Cursing the cops.

NOEL

The heat's because of the paintings. Why don't we take the fifty grand reward and maybe they'll let us go back to normal?

MARTIN

They're worth millions. I got lots of enquiries. Don't give in to them. What we gotta do is hit back. I'll get some lads, not on their list, to slash their tyres and scare their wives. I'll have their houses watched. We'll start with the top pricks – Kenny and O'Hara. See how they like it.

He rallies them. They cheer up at the prospect of going on the offensive but Gary is not convinced.

GARY

Them paintings is bad luck. I say get rid of them.

Martin hits Gary a vicious blow to the side of the head.

MARTIN

Don't you question my decisions. And sober up. And shut up.

Martin starts shaking. He grabs a bottle of soda pop and gulps it down. They watch him nervously as he looks up to address them. The smile has gone. They all recognize the look of danger in his eyes.

Go on as usual. And don't forget to draw yer dole. Otherwise they'll get yer on 'no visible means of support'.

INT. SWANN GROVE. FLAT. DAY

Martin is eating cake and watching television. Frances is walking up and down behind him holding Tina's arm. Tina holds her distended belly. She is having contractions. On the screen, the leader of one of the political parties, Des O'Malley, is addressing the Dáil.

O'MALLEY

There will be a new level of public cynicism when it becomes known that the notorious Martin Cahill has an eighty thousand-pound house as well as a corporation flat while every week drawing the dole.

Frances shakes Martin's shoulder as she passes.

85

FRANCES
Every five minutes. We should go.

Martin waves her away irritably.

O'MALLEY
I'm not entirely clear as to the reason for this, unless neither property is large enough on its own to hang his collection of paintings. Perhaps he needs the houses so that he can gaze at his collection of seventeenth-century Dutch masters.

Martin is enraged.

MARTIN
He can't accuse me of that. There's no evidence.

Tina gasps out a response.

TINA
He can, Martin. They can say what they like in the Dáil and get away with it.

MARTIN
Is that right? Why don't I get elected? I'd get the criminal vote. That's got to be fifty per cent of the country.

Tina leans on the sofa catching her breath.

TINA
You can't if you've got a criminal . . . ouch! . . . record.

MARTIN
How do you know all this?

TINA
School. You'd know if you'd ever gone.

Martin laughs, gets to his feet.

MARTIN
Ah, there's no justice. Come on. Let's get you to the hospital.

As they reach the door, Martin aims his zapper at the TV, but what he hears stops him in his tracks. Three faces stare back at the Newsreader, aghast.

NEWSREADER
(TV)

The Minister for Social Welfare, Michael Woods, has
announced that Cahill's unemployment assistance is being
suspended pending an investigation into his financial
situation. Mary Harney urged the Revenue Commissioners to
get involved. She reminded the Dáil that Al Capone was
jailed for tax evasion.

*Martin zaps the TV then throws the zapper at the set. He slams the
door behind him.*

EXT. SWANN GROVE. DAY

*The usual gauntlet of jeering cops to deal with. They jostle Martin and
the two women as they go to their car. 'Another little thief coming into
the world, Martin?' 'How many bastards will you have now?' Three
young hoods, Martin's B team, rush forward and barge the Gardai out
of the way. A Garda tackles one of the young criminals to the ground.
The others make their escape.*

Martin drives off, a police car closely following.

INT. CAHILL CAR. DAY

*Martin pulls up at a red light. The police car pulls up behind. It
deliberately gives them a shove, jerking them forward. Tina is jolted.
She turns round and shakes a fist. Martin is enraged.*

MARTIN
Every whoore in the land wants to bother me. Well, fuck
them all.

*The light changes. Martin drives on through a busy street. The police
car stays close on their tail.*

MARTIN
Hold tight, now.

He slams on his brakes. The police car rams into his rear.

Martin jumps out of the car. He appeals to the bystanders, screaming.

87

You saw that. I want compensation from the Gardai. I got a woman giving birth here and the cops harassing me.

He gets Tina out of the car. He rubs his neck.

And whiplash. Me neck is fucked.

People jeer at the cops. A youth bangs the police car with his fist. Martin opens the back door of the patrol car and shoves Tina in. He gets in after her. Frances climbs in the other side.

Right. Holles Street Maternity. And turn the siren on.

The cops are fuming, but they do as they are bid, taking orders from their quarry. Sitting back comfortably, Martin's smile returns.

EXT. COWPER DOWN HOUSE. DUSK

The surveillance team watches as Noel, Harry, Gary, Shea, Willy and Gay arrive at the front door. They ring the bell and steal shifty glances at the police. The door opens. Martin greets them with a big grin. He ushers them in.

INT. COWPER DOWN HOUSE. DUSK

Frances and Tina are tending to the baby. The gang members gather around it, making the oohs and aahs and other noises expected of them. The baby screams. Martin hands out clothes to each of the gang.

> MARTIN
> (*to Noel*)
> I got an offer for the paintings.

> NOEL
> Is it kosher, above board?

> MARTIN
> Let's find out.

EXT. COWPER DOWN. NIGHT

The Gardai are alerted as a balaclava-clad Martin Cahill emerges from his front door. Engines start up. On foot and by car, they prepare to follow.

Except that another Martin Cahill, identically dressed, face hidden by balaclava, steps out of the door and strides off in the opposite direction. The Gardai are perplexed. They split up to follow both as five Martin Cahills spill out of the house. Soon seven Martin Cahills are running in all directions. The Gardai, in disarray, call on their radios for reinforcements.

Somewhere among the seven men the real Martin Cahill has eluded them.

EXT. HOTEL. NIGHT

A car draws up at the entrance of a small hotel. Noel and Gary are in the front, still dressed as Martin lookalikes. Martin has been crouching in the back. He sits up and quickly gets out of the car and goes into the hotel.

INT. HOTEL. NIGHT

Martin is on the house phone.

MARTIN

Not in yer room. No. We'll do it down here.

He walks over and sits at a table in the bar. He studies his fellow customers.

Two men sit down with him, both Dutch. One of them (Blaankers) slides an envelope to him. Martin opens the flap just wide enough to satisfy himself that it is the promised wad of fifties. He pockets it.

BLAANKERS

Token of serious intent.
(*indicates his companion*)
This is Harry.

MARTIN

Your 'expert'.

Harry looks very nervous. He smiles at Martin. Both men are holding their room keys. The room numbers are clearly visible. Martin takes note.

BLAANKERS

You show him two paintings, the Vermeer being one of the two. If he is satisfied, half the money will be deposited in the Swiss bank as agreed. When you deliver the paintings, you get the other half. Now let's make a rendezvous for you and Harry.

Martin smells something. He studies the men at the bar. He's not sure.

MARTIN

I'll let yer know.

The waiter comes to their table.

I'll have a lemonade. Where's the gents'?

The waiter points the way. Martin gets up, leaves the bar.

INT. RECEPTION. NIGHT

Martin goes to the desk.

MARTIN

I want a room for the night.

RECEPTIONIST

What name would that be?

MARTIN

Kenny. Ned Kenny. I'll be paying cash.

He takes the envelope out of his pocket.

Back in the bar, the two Dutchmen glance at their watches, shrug. No sign of Martin.

INT. HOTEL CORRIDOR. DAY

Martin slips out of his room. He knocks on a door down the corridor. Harry opens the door. He is in his pyjamas.

MARTIN

Let's look at some pictures.

Harry's eyes roll in panic.

HARRY

I'll just let Blaankers know.

MARTIN

I don't think so.

EXT. STREET. DAY

Martin leads Harry to his Harley, one of the young hoods is waiting with it.

MARTIN

You didn't scratch it, did you?

Harry, still in pyjamas, gingerly climbs on to the pillion.

EXT. WICKLOW MOUNTAINS. DAY

Martin drives towards the copse which conceals the hiding place. He looks up. A helicopter in the sky. He grins.

EXT. COPSE. DAY

Much to Harry's discomfort, Martin drives through the copse over the rough terrain. He stops.

MARTIN

Pull that stone back. They're in there. I'll keep watch.

Harry goes over to the hiding place. Martin turns the bike and drives back to the road. He roars back the way he came. He looks back over his shoulder. The helicopter is coming down to land by the copse.

A police car comes racing up the road. Then another and another. Martin waves to them as they pass.

EXT. COPSE. DAY

Blaankers joins Harry from the helicopter. Police swarming everywhere. Harry's holding up an empty gilded picture frame.

HARRY

The frames are definitely genuine.

Higgins comes over to them.

HIGGINS

Well, that's a comfort.

BLAANKERS

Why would he bring you here?

HIGGINS

He's toying with us. It's his warped sense of humour. He's
showing off.

EXT. NOEL'S HOUSE. DAY

*Martin is outside the house sitting on the motorbike. Noel is standing
beside him. Martin grinning. Noel laughing. The Gardai in the patrol
car parked alongside are on the radio, clearly reporting Martin's visit.*

NOEL

They must have thought they had you.

MARTIN

We should think about moving them again soon.

Noel's mood darkens. He indicates to the ever-present cops.

> NOEL
>
> How can we with them climbing all over us?

> MARTIN
>
> Have fun with it. Make 'em suffer.

> NOEL
>
> Them paintings brought us bad luck, Martin. Let's get rid of
> them.

> MARTIN
>
> I've had another offer. From the Ulster Volunteer Force.

> NOEL
>
> Don't mess with them lads, Martin.

> MARTIN
>
> Why not? I don't give a fuck for them or the IRA.

> NOEL
>
> I can think of three reasons right off. They're from the North.
> They're Protestants. And they're terrorists. They're worse
> than us.

> MARTIN
> (*shrugs*)
>
> It's the only genuine offer I got.

*Martin starts the bike and roars off. The patrol car screeches after him,
but he is long gone.*

INT./EXT. COWPER DOWN HOUSE. DAY

*Tina, nursing her baby, watches from the window. A car draws up
outside and two men get out, Inspectors of the Revenue Commission.
Very much on their dignity, they walk up to the house escorted by two
Gardai.*

> TINA
>
> They're here, Martin.

Martin puts his head round the door.

MARTIN

Good. Show 'em in. Offer them a cuppa.

Later, Martin, the two men and Tina sit drinking their tea.

It's not my house. Belongs to my sister-in-law. She lets us
stay here sometimes.

REVENUE INSPECTOR I

You've made other substantial acquisitions we would like to
discuss with you. An expensive motorbike, for instance.

MARTIN

Oh, yer know, lucky day at the races. Would youse excuse me
for a minute. I got a bowel problem. Probably nerves. Yer
know, seeing youse an all.

*Martin goes out of the room. The two men smile at Tina. She smiles
back.*

TINA

More tea?

94

They decline

Do they pay you extra for making home visits?

They laugh politely.

REVENUE INSPECTOR 2
We do get a mileage allowance.

TINA
Oh. How much a mile?

REVENUE INSPECTOR 2
(*reluctantly*)
Seventy-five pence a mile, actually.

TINA
You must make a profit on that. And, of course, you pay tax
on it if you do, I'm sure.

They squirm in their seats. Martin returns.

MARTIN
I was thinking, sitting there in the khazi, that the whole of
Ireland's in the shit, yer know, what with drugs and vandals
and all. I put it down to a lack of respect for politician and
civil servants, people like that.

Something catches Martin's eye out of the window.

Look at that. Not your car I hope.

The Inspectors' car is ablaze.

See what I mean about these bloody vandals?

*The two men rush out. Martin's smile vanishes as soon as the front door
slams. His hands tremble and he is fighting for breath. He staggers
about the room. Tina is alarmed.*

TINA
Frances!

Frances appears from the kitchen followed by several children.

MARTIN

They'se all out to get me. I never should a bought this house
. . . We're not free any more like we were when we had
nothing . . .
(*leaning against the wall, panting*)
You lose yer dignity when you own things. You have to
defend them. You're a slave to the system.

*He lurches towards them, fighting for breath. The two women and four
children converge on him. They clutch him, support him, alarmed,
weeping.*

*Like a single creature they stagger around the room until Martin sinks
to the floor with his family folding in on him like petals.*

INT. BEDROOM. DAY

*Martin is in bed. A Doctor has just finished examining him. Frances
and Tina watch anxiously.*

DOCTOR

You'll learn how much insulin you need night and morning,
depending on how active you intend to be. Diabetes is
controllable if you're sensible.

Martin's grin returns.

MARTIN

And I used to be the one who didn't stick needles in himself.

*The irony appeals to him. The Doctor packs his bag. Frances leans
down to kiss Martin.*

Yer beat the whole world, then yer own body turns on yer.
It's a bollix.

The Doctor turns at the door.

DOCTOR

And no more cream cakes.

Martin groans.

EXT. ALLEY. DAY (DREAM)

The alley is endless. Junk, burning tyres, derelict houses. Twelve-year-old Martin is running. Cops chasing. His two brothers have fallen behind. He looks back, sees his brothers grabbed by the cops, keeps running on alone.

INT. BEDROOM. DAY

Martin opens his eyes. Frances is sitting by the bed.

> FRANCES
>
> Noel is here.

Noel is standing by the bedroom door. He steps over awkwardly to the bedside. Frances leaves the room.

> NOEL
>
> How you keeping, Martin?

> MARTIN
>
> Never better. Listen. I want you to ride shotgun tomorrow when I meet these UVF bollix.

Noel looks painfully uncomfortable.

> NOEL
>
> I can't. I'm in court tomorrow.

> MARTIN
>
> For what? Yer never got nicked, did yer?

> NOEL
>
> I confessed to that post office job. I have to get away from the strain of it. I need a few months inside. I need the rest. Recuperation. I've lost me appetite for crime.

> MARTIN
>
> Jaysus. Noel. Yer all deserting me. They picked up Shea and Jimmy – careless, they were. They're in court next week.

Noel cannot meet Martin's look.

> NOEL
>
> You better have this yoke. Key to the garage.

97

He tosses the key to Martin. He sighs. He has more bad news. Should he tell it now?

> MARTIN
>
> Something else you want to tell me?

Noel nods, takes a deep breath.

> NOEL
>
> They shot Willy last night. He was doing a stroke. Only a supermarket. He snuck out late. Thought he'd slipped surveillance. All he was after was food for the kids. If it had been open he would have paid for it with his own money.
>> *(there's a catch in his voice)*
>
> They shot him dead coming out. The Garda have got more guns than we have now. It's getting decidedly hazardous to ply our trade.

Martin becomes very pensive but shows no other emotion.

> MARTIN
>
> I got no one left.

> NOEL
>
> You got plenty of young fellas. They worship you. They'd die for yer. They'd welcome a martyr's death.

> MARTIN
>
> But you're the last one from Hollyfield. The only ones I can trust are Hollyfield lads.
>> *(he smiles, thinking back)*
>
> We had some *craic*, didn't we, as kids?

> NOEL
>
> There's Gary.

> MARTIN
>> *(grins)*
>
> Yeah. There's Gary.

Noel, overcome, impetuously embraces Martin.

Eh, we're not fucking Italians.

He shoves Noel away in a good-natured manner.

INT./EXT. COWPER DOWN. LIVING-ROOM. NIGHT

The room is unlit. Martin is standing in the window with a fervent young man, Aidan. Two Gardai sit in their patrol car outside.

AIDAN
We nicked some dynamite from the quarry. Can we use dynamite?

MARTIN
No. These are neighbours of mine. Just smash their windows, slash a few tyres. Cause a diversion is all.

EXT. COWPER DOWN. NIGHT

The surveillance cops react to sounds of breaking glass and screams for help.

They leave their post and run down the road. One of the enthusiastic youths has set a house on fire.

Martin slips out of the house and melts into the shadows.

EXT./INT. GARAGE. NIGHT

Martin studies the Vermeer. Shakes his head, can't figure it out. He rolls it up and slides it back into its plastic tube. He picks up one of the other rolled-up paintings and locks the garage. It is one of a group of garages behind a block of flats.

INT. GARY'S HOUSE. NIGHT

Gary sits at the kitchen table drinking beer. Martin is across from him. He cradles the painting on his lap. Gary's fourteen-year-old daughter, Maeve, is at the sink. Two toddlers are whining at her feet.

GARY
Get them out of here, Maeve. You can see I'm busy.

Maeve hoists them up and bundles them out of the room.

MARTIN
Has she looked after them on her own since the mammy died?

GARY

Won't do her no harm. The granny comes up in the day.

Martin looks around carefully at the slovenly room.

MARTIN

You don't have surveillance, Gary?

GARY

No. They gave up on me.

MARTIN

Do you still have that foldaway piece?

GARY

Yeah. Under the floorboards.

MARTIN

Get it.

INT. WAREHOUSE. NIGHT

Martin and Gary descend narrow stone steps. Martin probes the darkness with a flashlight.

GARY

Is this it? I don't like it.

MARTIN

Keep out of sight till I call you.

Martin advances into the domed warehouse, searching the shadows. There are holes in the ceiling at regular intervals which allow columns of light to fall below.

A figure moves into a distant shaft and is gone again. Martin moves toward it. He stops. The figure steps into the light again for an instant and gestures Martin to come forward.

Martin moves towards the shaft of light and scans the walls with his lamp, catching glimpses and shapes of several men.

A VOICE

Turn it off.

Martin shrugs, switching off the flashlight. He steps into the edge of the shaft of light. He is aware of several figures. The Leader steps forward into the outer edge of the shaft of light.

                              LEADER
Are you a Republican, Cahill?

                              MARTIN
Criminal. What are you?

                              LEADER
Loyalists.

                              MARTIN
I'm all for loyalty. Who youse loyal to?

                              LEADER
The Queen.

                              MARTIN
Great. I identify with her. Her ancestors tortured and
murdered and grabbed what they wanted and she don't pay
no taxes. She's my hero.

                              LEADER
You're very sure of yourself.

                              MARTIN
Well, I've got cover.

*He shines his torch at the arch where Gary watches. Gary and his gun
are lit up for an instant. The other Loyalists tense up. The Leader nods
at the rolled-up painting.*

                              LEADER
Is that it?

*Martin unfurls the painting enough to reveal the head and breasts of the
Rubens nude.*

                              MARTIN
Yeah. Sample of my wares.

*Martin hands it over. The Leader gives him a slip of paper. Martin
squints at it.*

A South African bank?

LEADER

That's where our weapons are coming from. Your money's there. Once they authenticate the painting.

MARTIN

Well, I trust you.

LEADER

And why's that, Cahill?

MARTIN

If you let me down, I'll tell the Queen.

EXT. REAR OF COWPER DOWN HOUSE. NIGHT

A Garda is up in a tree overlooking the garden and the lane behind it. He sweeps the house and garden with night binoculars.

We see the infrared image moving across the terrain. As it reaches the lane, a form can be discerned crawling slowly on its belly towards the fence.

The Garda switches on his flashlight. It illuminates Martin moving towards a hole at the bottom of the fence.

Martin freezes when the light comes on.

The Garda speaks quietly into his walkie-talkie.

> GARDA
>
> Tango One just crept out from under a stone.

He keeps the beam on Martin who does not move. Another Garda appears in the lane.

He leans over and points his torch at Martin whose face is pressed into the ground.

> GARDA 2
>
> You're creepy and you're crawly, Cahill, you fucking slug.

No movement or response from Martin. The Garda pisses on him.

Later: the first Garda climbs down from the tree. The sun is coming up.

He goes over to Martin who is still prone and motionless.

Tommy appears in the pigeon loft, feeding the birds.

> GARDA
> (*voice-over*)
>
> Get up Cahill, you filthy knacker.

Tommy looks up. He jumps down from the loft and runs to the end of the garden.

> TOMMY
>
> Da. Is that you, Da?

He looks over the fence.

> What yer doin', Da?

Martin jumps to his feet and hops over into the garden.

> MARTIN
>
> It was a nice night, son. I had a notion to sleep outside.

It's fucking freezing.

Martin cuffs him.

MARTIN

Watch yer language. This is a respectable neighbourhood, worse fucking luck.

INT. KITCHEN. COWPER DOWN HOUSE. DAY

Martin looks ill. He is trying to warm himself in front of the kitchen stove. He is shaking all over. Frances gives him an injection of insulin. Tommy hands his father a cup of tea.

FRANCES

Are yer outa yer mind, Martin?

MARTIN

I don't want them to know they're bothering me. It's a game.

FRANCES

Yer murdering yerself with yer pride.

The surveillance team are shouting insults outside.

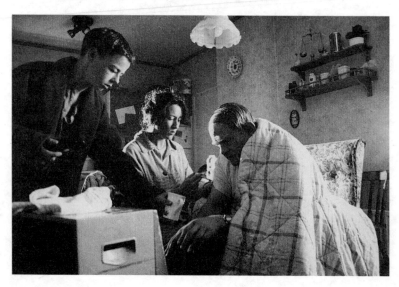

GARDA
(*voice-over*)
Turn the radio on, Cahill.

Frances switches it on.

NEWSREADER
. . . this is the first of Sir Alfred Beit's paintings to be
recovered. Three men, members of the terrorist organization
the Ulster Volunteer Force were arrested in possession of the
painting in a sting operation involving the police forces of . . .

*Martin looks stricken. Frances is anxious and perplexed. Martin grits
his teeth.*

MARTIN
Come on, son. Finish feeding the pigeons.

He gets painfully to his feet. The show must go on.

EXT. COWPER DOWN HOUSE. DAY

*An ironic cheer goes up from the surveillance team as Martin and his
son appear in the pigeon loft. A Garda is sitting on the garden wall,*

another in the tree, two more look over the fence at the end of the garden. They start to chant 'Traitor', 'Traitor'.

'Don't Fence Me In' blares out.

Detective Sergeant Higgins appears, climbing on to the wall from the next-door garden.

> HIGGINS
> We've got you now, Cahill. I didn't think even you would sink this low. Your neighbours'll lynch you when they find out you're dealing with the Proddies.

Tommy starts taking photos of the Gardai. Gardai throw stones and jeer as Martin fondles his birds. Martin turns to face them. He has a big grin on his face.

> MARTIN
> Get off me wall, Higgins, or I'll call the cops.

Tommy loves the joke. He is laughing his head off. Arm in arm, they go back into the house.

EXT. DUBLIN CANAL. DAY

Martin drives up on his Harley. Gary is waiting for him, pacing, wringing his hands. As Martin dismounts, a patrol car draws up behind him. Martin goes to Gary. Two patrolmen get out of the car and follow. Gary's face is twisted with anguish.

> GARY
> Shit. They followed yer.

> MARTIN
> I didn't have time to slip them. You were that desperate. What is it?

The Gardai are only three paces away, staring and grinning at the encounter. Gary holds Martin by the shoulders and whispers in his ear.

> GARY
> I can't tell yer with them watching.

They look like lovers clasped together.

I can tell you what's bothering him. He's been charged.
Raping and buggering his fourteen-year-old daughter. That's
the man you're holding in your arms, you poof.

Martin reflexively shoves Gary away from him.

MARTIN

Yer did that, yer bollix?

*Martin shoves him towards the road. He strides after him, pushing him
ahead, jabbing him in the back. The Gardai follow. Martin sees a bus
slowing as it comes to the bridge crossing the canal. Along the side of the
bus is a sign:* LITERARY TOUR OF DUBLIN.

Run, you prick.

*Martin scampers for the bus and jumps on. Gary sprints alongside it as
it pulls away and scrambles on, landing on his knees.*

The Gardai run back for their car.

INT. BUS. DAY

*There are only a handful of tourists on the lower deck. The two men
slump into a seat. Martin is having a problem getting his breath back
and he is in a fury.*

GUIDE
(*voice-over*)

Although *Ulysses* describes every inch of Dublin, Joyce himself
fled to Paris, escaping what he called 'the daily spite of this
unmannered city'. To the right is the home of Oliver St John
Gogarty, the famous wit who once said . . .
(*and so on*)

MARTIN

You're a gobshite. Criminals don't molest kids. Leave that to
the priests, you scum.

GARY

If I did that I'll kill myself. It was after that night with the
Proddies. Me nerves was in pieces. I got dead drunk. I forgot
me wife was dead. I thought it was her. I dunno what I did to

Maeve. You've gotta help me, Martin. The Gardai'll beat the shite out of me – you know what they're like with perverts – and I don't know what I'd say, I'd be in that much of a state.

He is blubbering and weeping. Martin looks at him with disgust.

GUIDE
(*voice-over*)
Beckett soon left for Paris too and never came back. Many Irish writers – Oscar Wilde, Bernard Shaw – got out as soon as they could. Now, of course, writers live tax free in this country, and nobody leaves any more.

EXT. BACK GARDEN. DAY

A tough-looking woman is pegging out clothes on the washing line in her narrow back garden. She is Mrs Duggan, Gary's mother-in-law and Maeve's grandmother.

Martin hops over the wall and comes up stealthily behind the woman. She does not appear to see him, certainly does not acknowledge his presence, but –

Save yer breath to cool your porridge, Martin Cahill.

MARTIN

I condemn him for what he done. I curse him, Mrs Duggan.
May he die roaring for a priest. But don't turn that girl into a
tout. You're from Hollyfield. Hollyfield people don't go to
the cops. We settle things ourselves. You're betraying
everything we stand for.

MRS DUGGAN
(*turns on him, raging*)
What? What do you stand for? Thieving and killing and
scaring people to death? Well, we don't live in Hollyfield now,
thank God.

MARTIN
(*a weary threat in his voice*)
Think what you're saying, Mrs Duggan.

MRS DUGGAN

You can't scare me. I lost me daughter. I seen this happen to
me granddaughter. Kill me. You'd be doing me a favour.

*Martin seems to have little enthusiasm for his mission. His attention is
taken by a sheet flapping on the line. The wind rattles it against his
face. He holds it and nostalgically inhales its fragrance.*

MARTIN
(*with regret*)
We got a washer–dryer now.

*Maeve appears from the house with another bundle of washing,
breaking Martin's reverie. He leans in to Mrs Duggan.*

Here's me offer. I'll buy her a little house. And twenty grand
to help her along. She'll be under my protection. And her
uncles can give Gary a lashing.

*Mrs Duggan looks at him with disdain. Martin gives Maeve a smile.
She looks past him. She seems numb and expressionless.*

Hello, Maeve. I've come to give you a hand. Sorry for yer

troubles. Yer nana will tell you what me offer is. Think about it. I know you don't want to be a tout.

He backs away. Maeve and Mrs Duggan busy themselves with the laundry. Martin climbs over the fence and is gone.

EXT. COWPER DOWN HOUSE. DAY

Martin climbs over the fence into his back garden. He finds Sergeant Higgins sitting on the wall that separates Martin's garden from his neighbour's.

> HIGGINS
> You stay away from Mrs Duggan or we'll have you on perverting the course of justice. You'd get ten years for that. We don't have to bother following you any more. Your own kind are reporting on you.

> MARTIN
> Get off my wall. You're trespassing.

> HIGGINS
> It's a party wall. And Mrs Harney's having a party. She invited us in.

Martin climbs up to his pigeon loft where he can overlook his neighbour's garden. Mrs Harney is bringing cups of tea to several Gardai who lounge in her garden. In one of her windows facing on to the Cahill house, a Garda is watching him through binoculars.

Martin nips into the house and emerges with a loud hailer.

> MARTIN
>
> Get those cops out of yer place, Mrs Harney, or I'll burn them out. I'm warning yer. If you want to live next to me, if you want to stay alive, toss those whoores out a there.

> HIGGINS
>
> That's it, Cahill. We're taking you in.

INT. GARDA INTERVIEW ROOM. NIGHT

Martin is being grilled by Higgins and two other detectives.

> HIGGINS
>
> I like you, Martin. God knows why, but there's nothing I can do for you here. Look at your situation. Gary will talk, I guarantee. Those three UVF fellas, we'll make them a deal to testify against you . . . and the IRA are not going to be too happy about you helping the Loyalists to buy weapons.

> MARTIN
>
> Where's me lawyer? Higgins is a queer. Higgins shags sheep. Higgins is a wanker. Higgins is a child molester.

> HIGGINS
>
> The shit's up to your neck and rising. Is it time for other means, Martin? You know my methods.

Kenny enters the room.

> KENNY
>
> Out, Pat, I'll take him.

Higgins and the two cops start to leave.

> HIGGINS
>
> I'll be outside. How's your pigeons, Martin?

MARTIN

Bye bye, Higgins, bye bye, Higgins, bye bye, Higgins.

Martin stares at the wall.

KENNY

Martin, you're in a deep, deep hole. I'm gonna put you away. I'm stitching you up for your own good.

MARTIN

Kenny is a murderer, he's gonna frame me. Kenny's gonna stitch me. He's gonna plant something on me. He's threatening me.

KENNY

Martin, listen to me, can't you see it? There's a bullet coming. Can't you smell it, can't you feel it? Listen to me, you fuck . . .

Kenny hits Martin.

MARTIN

Stop hitting me, please.

Kenny stops hitting Martin and goes quiet.

See, your mistake is, you're doing stuff to me that would bother you. Well, I'm not like you. It's water off a duck's back. But I tell yer what, you're getting to be like me. Trespass, intimidation, harassing. You've had to come down to my level.

KENNY

That's right, you've brought me down with you. I'm in the gutter as well.

MARTIN

You used to be a straight cop. A good culshie boy from Kerry. Always did what the priest told you. Knew right from wrong. Now you got the press and the politicians on yer back, yer church has let yer down so yer don't even feel bad about it. Nobody believes in nothing any more. 'Cept me.

KENNY

Would it suit you if it was my bullet?

INT. DISTRICT COURT. DAY

Martin is in the dock with his solicitor, Lawrence Lawless. He is wearing a moustache and beard from a joke shop and a pair of glasses with eyes painted on them. Detective Sergeant Higgins is on the witness stand. Kenny stands at the back of the court in whispered conference with a severe-looking Garda Commissioner, Reynolds.

JUDGE

Sergeant, can you identify the accused despite the silly disguise?

HIGGINS

Yes, sir. He is Martin Cahill.

Later: Martin is on the stand.

JUDGE

Do you give an undertaking to desist from threatening your neighbour.

MARTIN

I do. And will you tell Inspector Kenny to stop threatening me?

113

The Judge sighs.

JUDGE

You are bound over to keep the peace.

EXT. DISTRICT COURT. DAY

Martin pulls a balaclava over his face as he emerges to face a barrage of press and television reporters. Questions fly at him. 'Where are the Beit paintings?' 'Why are you dealing with terrorists?' and a chorus of 'Show yourself' from the photographers and TV cameramen.

MARTIN

Show meself?

Martin throws off his anorak and twirls around, wiggling his hips like a striptease dancer. He wears the usual Mickey Mouse T-shirt. He unzips his jeans and they drop to his ankles revealing garishly coloured boxer shorts. What he does not show is his face. The crowd presses in on him.

Kenny and Reynolds, leaving the court, find their exit blocked by the tumult.

114

REYNOLDS
He's making a horse's arse of you.

KENNY
Give me another month, sir. He's cracking.

Several of Martin's young hoods push through to his rescue. They surround him and guide him towards a waiting car. With his jeans hobbling his ankles he finds it difficult to walk. They pick him up and carry him, like a sporting hero, and, indeed, Martin waves to the crowd. Kenny and Reynolds watch despairingly.

REYNOLDS
Cracking up?

INT. GARY'S HOUSE. NIGHT

Martin taps on the kitchen door. Gary, looking a mess, lets him in.

GARY
It's tomorrow, Martin. She's determined to testify.

Martin thinks it over.

MARTIN
Didn't that parish priest do you when you were an altar boy.

GARY
Yeah. He done all of us lads.

MARTIN
You can use that for yer defence. Yer know, you can say it screwed up yer sex life.

GARY
Ah, I wouldn't want to grass on him. He was a nice old boy. It didn't hurt that much and he enjoyed it. And he let us drink the altar wine.

Martin paces the room. He looks edgy.

MARTIN
If we can get it adjourned for three months, it'll give her time to change her mind.

GARY

We've tried every avenue.

Martin ponders. They fall silent.

MARTIN

There's one thing we can do.

Martin pulls out a revolver.

Stage a break in. Rough the place up a bit. I give you a flesh wound. That'll do it.

GARY

You think so?

MARTIN

Yeah. They'll have to delay it.

Gary looks less than happy at the prospect.

GARY

Let me have a drink to dull the pain.

He reaches for the Paddy whiskey and slugs it out of the bottle. Martin starts smashing crockery and turning over furniture with an angry violence far beyond what is necessary.

Ah, Jaysus, Martin, that was me favourite mug.

Martin takes a chair and goes into the living-room. Gary winces at the sounds of destruction.

Martin returns.

MARTIN

Now. Stand up, Gary, so I can get a look at yer leg.

Gary takes more whiskey as he gets to his feet. He looks ruefully at the gun which Martin is holding rather shakily. Martin brings the gun within inches of Gary's leg. He moves the gun up towards the knee. He fires. Gary screams in agony.

GARY

You've smashed me kneecap, Martin!

Martin offers his mock innocent face.

> MARTIN
>
> Jaysus! Sorry, Gary. Me aim's all to fuck since I got this diabolicals. Mind, it'll look more genuine.

Gary hops around the room in paroxysms of pain. Martin goes to the door.

> Give me a few minutes then call the ambulance and the cops. Good luck, Gary.

INT. CAHILL BEDROOM. DAY

Frances, fully dressed, comes in to wake Martin. She has his insulin syringe. He sits up in the bed, yawning. He wears only his boxer shorts. Frances looks nervous.

> MARTIN
>
> What's wrong?

> FRANCES
>
> Do your insulin.

Martin takes the syringe and prepares to inject it into his abdomen.

117

MARTIN

Come on. What's wrong?

FRANCES

It was on the radio. They found the paintings.

Martin jabs the syringe viciously into his abdomen.

MARTIN

They couldn't have. Only Noel and me knew . . . Noel! He
touted on me. That's why he wanted to go inside. He knew
I'd kill him. Fucking traitor.

*He jumps to his feet. The syringe is hanging out of his stomach, flapping
about. He runs out into the living-room. Frances hurries after him.*

INT. LIVING-ROOM. DAY

MARTIN

They're all ratting on me.

He flings the syringe away.

FRANCES

No, Martin. There was a fire in the next garage. The fire
brigade opened it up. It was just bad luck.

*Martin is staring wild-eyed, in the grips of paranoia. He paces around
as though searching the house for hidden enemies. Tina's baby screams
at the sight of him.*

MARTIN

You believe that? They're putting that out to protect Noel.

FRANCES

Noel wouldn't.

MARTIN

I can trust no one. Where's Tina? I saw her talking to a cop
yesterday. I won't have that.

*He sees something out of the front window. The Tango team saunters up
and down. Two of the Cahill children are playing in the street. There
are other children.*

118

EXT. COWPER DOWN HOUSE. DAY

Still only in boxer shorts, Martin runs out into the front garden. He glimpses Sergeant Higgins carrying a sack into Mrs Harney's house.

MARTIN

Get inside, you two.

The children come trotting in.

INT. LIVING-ROOM. DAY

Martin slaps the children around their heads. They wail. Their mother gathers them in her arms.

MARTIN

I've told yer. Yer don't play with the neighbours' kids.

GIRL
(*through her tears*)
You don't have to worry, Da. They won't play with us.

Martin slumps down into an armchair and buries his head in his hands. Frances comforts him.

EXT. CAHILL GARDEN. DAY

Sergeant Higgins peers over the party wall, makes sure he is not observed, then opens his sack and pulls out a weasel. It wriggles and struggles, snapping at his hand.

INT. BEDROOM. DAY

Martin is dressing, pulling on his Mickey Mouse T-shirt. He has calmed down. Frances approaches him tentatively.

FRANCES

Let's go out tonight. Just you and me and Tina. Go to a restaurant. Show them they're not getting to us.

Martin grimly nods his assent.

Go on with you. Feed yer pigeons.

INT. PIGEON LOFT. DAY

The door opens to reveal Martin and his son. The weasel scurries under their feet and out of the open door. The pigeons are all dead. Martin's face trembles with anguish. He fights to control his feelings. Tommy bursts into tears. Martin grips his son by the shoulder.

> MARTIN
> Stop it. Stop that bawling. We're going outside in a moment. They'll all be watching. I want you to smile, you hear?

The boy nods his head but he is sobbing. He wipes his eyes on his sleeve.

> Smile, you little prick.

EXT. PIGEON LOFT. DAY

Martin and his son emerge. The Tango squad starts jeering, then falls silent as they see the man and boy appearing to share a joke. Martin and Tommy throw back their heads and laugh and laugh.

INT. RESTAURANT. NIGHT

Martin sits between his two women. Two cops eat at another table.

The waiter brings the dessert trolley. Martin ogles the cream cakes and profiteroles. Reluctantly, he shakes his head.

> MARTIN
> Them days is gone for ever.

> FRANCES
> Remember when you stole me a cream cake. What was I, ten?

> MARTIN
> I loved yer then and I love yer still. They were good times.

> TINA
> Where was I?

> MARTIN
> Probably crapping in yer nappy.

They have a good laugh.

FRANCES

It's Us against Them, you said.

MARTIN

Still is.

Frances takes his hand. Tina takes the other.

INT. COWPER DOWN HOUSE. DAY

Frances, in her dressing-gown, is looking out of the window into the street.

FRANCES

Martin. Come and look.

Martin ambles to the window. He is dressed.

No cops. You've beaten them.

She gives him a hug, but Martin eyes the empty street with suspicion.

EXT. COWPER DOWN HOUSE. DAY

Martin comes out of the house and goes to his car. He stops, sniffs the air. He looks up and down the street. Deserted. Except for a corporation worker with a clipboard at the end of the street ticking off the passing cars.

INT. CAR. DAY

He drives down to the end of the road and pulls up at the stop sign.

The 'corporation worker' is sprinting towards him. He is pointing a silver-plated Magnum at the car. Martin looks into the face of his nemesis.

The gun is moving extremely slowly towards the side window.

EXT. ALLEY. DAY

The young Martin runs down the endless alley. He looks back, grinning at his pursuers, then runs on and on.

INT. CAR. DAY

The ghost of a grin on Martin's face.

The gun is almost touching the window when it fires. There is no sound.

The window splinters into an opaque pattern that obscures the assassin. It fills the screen. There is a tiny hole in the middle.

Fade out.

CREDITS

Martin Cahill	BRENDAN GLEESON
Noel Curley	ADRIAN DUNBAR
Gary	SEAN MCGINLEY
Frances	MARIA DOYLE KENNEDY
Tina	ANGELINE BALL
Inspector Ned Kenny	JON VOIGHT
Jimmy	EANNA MCLIAM
Willy Byrne	TOM MURPHY
Anthony	PAUL HICKEY
Paddy	TOMMY O'NEILL
Shea	JOHN O'TOOLE
Tommy	CIARAN FITZGERALD
Gay	NED DENNEHY
Harry	VINNIE MURPHY
Orla	ROXANNA WILLIAMS
Young Martin Cahill	EAMON OWENS
Patricia	COLLEEN O'NEILL
Sylvie	MAEBH GORBY
Higgins	PAT LAFFAN
Lawless	FRANK MELIA
James Donovan	RONAN WILMOT
Arcade Woman	LYNN CAHILL
Assassin	DAVID WILMOT
Arthur Ryan	STEPHEN BRENNAN
Henry Mackie	DON WICHERLEY
Judge	KEVIN FLOOD
Desk Guard	PAT KINEVANE
IRA Leader	BARRY MCGOVERN
Mrs Duggan	PAT LEAVY
Maeve	NEILE CONROY
Beavis	PETER HUGO DALY
Young Frances	AOIFE MORIARITY
UVF Leader	BRENDAN COYLE
CPAD Leader	JIM SHERIDAN

Young Hood # 1	GAVIN KELTY
Revenue Men	OWEN O'NEILL
	DAVID CAREY
Reporters	NIAMH LINEHAN
	JASON BYRNE
TV Newsreader	ANN DOYLE
Young Detective	DARAGH KELLY
Des O'Malley	HIMSELF

CREW

Produced, Written & Directed by	John Boorman
Executive Producer	Kieran Corrigan
Director of Photography & Camera Operator	Seamus Deasy
Production Design	Derek Wallace
Music Composer	Richie Buckley
Editor	Ron Davis
Costume Design	Maeve Paterson
Casting Director	Jina Jay
Production Manager	Jo Homewood
1st Assistant Director	Kevan Barker
Location Manager	Mick Walsh
Production Accountant	Con Cremins
Assistant to John Boorman	Sonya Supple
Script Supervisor	Laerke Sigfred Petersen
Focus Puller	Shane Deasy
Clapper/Loader	Simon Walsh
Key Grip	John Murphy
Gaffer	Noel Cullen
Best Boy	Kieran Dempsey
Sound Recordist	Brendan Deasy
Boom Operator	Eddie Quinn
Special Effects	Team FX
2nd Assistant Director	Paul Barnes
3rd Assistant Director	Paddy McCarney
Production Co-ordinator	Carol Moorhead
Production Secretary	Rachel Smith
Prop Master	Paul Hedges
Set Dresser	Shirley Henderson
Assistant Art Director	Irene O'Brien
Paintings by	Jill Andrea Reid

Assistant Editor	Bob Robinson
Re-recording Mixer	Douglas E. Turner
Head Make-up Artist	Maire O'Sullivan
Head Hairdresser	Orla Carroll
Assistant Make-up Artist	Lynn Johnston
Assistant Hairdresser	Conor McAlistair
Wardrobe Mistress	Margaret Crosse
Wardrobe Assistants	Susan O'Connor Cave
	Fiona Whelan
Dialogue Coach	Poll Moussoulides
Assistant Casting Director	Chloe Emerson
Stills Photographer	Pat Redmond
Action Vehicles	Stephen Carroll
Construction Supervisor	Dave Wheelan